PENGUIN BOOKS

TALKING OF LOVE

Boris Cyrulnik is an internationally renowned psychologist and leading proponent of the theory of resilience: that we are much more capable of overcoming traumatic events in our lives than we imagine. Working with genocide victims in Rwanda and child soldiers in Colombia, he travels around the world helping individuals and countries come to terms with their pasts to create positive new outlooks. He is the author of numerous books on resilience (including *Resilience*, also published by Penguin) and its possibilities in childhood and throughout life. An international bestseller, his work has been credited with helping France heal the wounds left by the Second World War. Cyrulnik was born in 1937; in 1942 his parents were deported to a concentration camp and never returned. Maltreated by his foster parents, he was eventually chosen to be a runner in the liberation, perilously crossing enemy lines to deliver messages to French fighters. He was seven. This personal trauma helped him develop his belief that trauma is not destiny.

21 Aug 09

to my 11p,

I saw this and thought of us, as the last few years have been quite traumatic!!

Whenever you feel 'down', read this and remind yourself how much worse it could ~~be be~~ be.

Or read it and laugh at its awfulness. Or it may even help — who knows?!

If all else fails use it for fire wood in the winter!

This book is for no more rubbish boys and no more heartache! Amen sista (gangster).

Love forever and always, your completely emotionally independent

Talking of Love

How to Overcome Trauma and Remake Your Life Story

Boris Cyrulnik

TRANSLATED BY
DAVID MACEY

PENGUIN BOOKS

BF, Stephanie x x x

PENGUIN BOOKS

Published by the Penguin Group
Penguin Books Ltd, 80 Strand, London WC2R ORL, England
Penguin Group (USA) Inc., 375 Hudson Street, New York, New York 10014, USA
Penguin Group (Canada), 90 Eglinton Avenue East, Suite 700, Toronto, Ontario, Canada M4P 2Y3
(a division of Pearson Penguin Canada Inc.)
Penguin Ireland, 25 St Stephen's Green, Dublin 2, Ireland (a division of Penguin Books Ltd)
Penguin Group (Australia), 250 Camberwell Road, Camberwell, Victoria 3124, Australia
(a division of Pearson Australia Group Pty Ltd)
Penguin Books India Pvt Ltd, 11 Community Centre, Panchsheel Park, New Delhi – 110 017, India
Penguin Group (NZ), 67 Apollo Drive, Rosedale, North Shore 0632, New Zealand
(a division of Pearson New Zealand Ltd)
Penguin Books (South Africa) (Pty) Ltd, 24 Sturdee Avenue, Rosebank,
Johannesburg 2196, South Africa

Penguin Books Ltd, Registered Offices: 80 Strand, London WC2R ORL, England

www.penguin.com

First published in France as *Parler d'Amour au bord de gouffre* 2005
First published in Great Britain as *Talking of Love on the Edge of a Precipice* 2007
Published in Penguin Books 2009

1

Ouvrage publié avec le concours du Ministère français chargé de la culture –
Centre nationale du livre

Published with the support of the French Ministry of Culture / Centre nationale du livre

Typeset in 14/16.15 pt Fournier
Set by Palimpsest Book Production Limited, Grangemouth, Stirlingshire
Printed in England by Clays Ltd, St Ives plc

978-0-141-02579-7

www.greenpenguin.co.uk

Contents

I Introduction

II Resilience as Anti-Destiny

Contents

III When a Meeting Is a Reunion

Contents

IV The Metaphysics of Love

V Inheriting Hell

Contents

VI Sombre Songs

VII Conclusion

*Resilience avoids identification with either the
aggressor or the victim of the aggression. Love
is a third way, and it is much more constructive.*

I

Introduction

An Innocent Helper

If you want to look wise, all you have to do is keep quiet. But when you are sixteen, even chatting is like verbal mating: you're dying to talk.

I don't remember his first name. We called him 'Rouland', which was his surname, I think. He never said anything, but he had his own way of saying nothing. For some people, saying nothing is a way of hiding. They hang their heads and avoid other people's eyes in order to cut themselves off. But when this young man put on his sombre look, it was his way of saying: 'I'm watching you and I'm interested in you, but I'm keeping quiet so as not to give myself away.'

I was captivated by Rouland because he could run fast. That was important to the Lycée Jacques Decours's junior rugby team. Although physical strength often allowed us to dominate the game, we used to lose because we did not have a fast winger. So I made friends with him. During our conversations, I had to do all the work: questions, answers, initiatives, decisions about training. One day, he suddenly said to me after a long silence: 'My mother's invited you to tea.'

At the top of the rue Victor-Massé, near Pigalle, there was a cul-de-sac. It was like a village, with rough cobbles, fruit and vegetable stalls and a charcuterie. On the second floor there was a bijou flat. Rouland sat in silence on a sofa. I was stuffed with chocolate, cake and candied fruit, all served on little plates with gilt edges. Was I trying hard to pretend that I didn't know how his mother made her living in the rue Victor-Massé and the bars of Pigalle?

Fifty years later – just a few months ago – I had a phone call. 'It's Rouland. I'm in your area. Could I see you for a few minutes?' He was slim, smart, quite good looking and a lot more talkative than he used to be. 'I went to business school. Business never interested me very much, but I preferred the company of books to that of friends who bored me and girls who terrified me. I wanted to tell you that you changed my life.' 'Good God!' I thought. He went on: 'I want to thank you for pretending not to know what my mother did for a living.' He couldn't bring himself to say the word. 'It was the first time I'd seen anyone show her any consideration. For years, I used to run the film through my mind: you acting innocent, a little too polite, perhaps, but it was the first time anyone had shown my mother any respect. That was the day when I regained hope. I wanted you to know that.'

Although he had changed for the better, Rouland was still boring. We never saw each other again, but that encounter set me thinking. Living in my own little world, all I'd wanted to do was recruit him as a wing three-quarter for the rugby team. I had no reason to despise that nice lady, even if she was strangely dressed. But in his little world, this incident had caused an upheaval. It had done him good. He had discovered that he did not have to be ashamed. With a third party looking on, he began to feel less tormented by what his mother did for a living and it was beginning to look as if he might find some inner peace. The psychological work remained to be done, but he was beginning to believe that it could be done because he had just realized that we can change the way we feel. My bad play-acting had acted out a meaning that was important to him. In my bored politeness, I had given him a little hope.

The two of us ascribed different meanings to the same behavioural scenario. They lay not in anything that was said or done, but in our private histories: for me, it was a minor incident, but for him it was an emotional upheaval. Fifty years later, I learned to my astonishment that I had acted as Rouland's resilience tutor.

He believed in the light because he was living in the dark. Because I was living in full daylight, I could not see anything.[1] I had perceived something real that did not mean much to me. A lady gave me too many chocolates. It was hot in her flat and I wondered how she could breathe in a sheath that was so close fitting her breasts strained against it. Being a prisoner of the present, I was fascinated, but Rouland was living through a foundational moment.

The Annunciation of Olga

Olga sighs. 'At quarter to eight yesterday, a single sentence made my soul ache: "You might never walk again." Before the accident, my life was just a succession of grey days. I was having a dreary time of it at university, with just a day's skiing or a night of techno to liven things up from time to time. At quarter to eight, just one sentence tore my world apart. Someone had said it. At first, I was so numb that I felt no pain. It was only later that the agony began, and I realized that I hadn't lived my life to the full. "It's so stupid. I should have had more good times. I should have enjoyed every second of my life." "What do you want from me?" asked the doctor. "The truth," I said. But I was lying. There was just a chance that this was a bad dream. The last thing I wanted was to dash that hope. The truth is that I was hoping he would say it was just a bad dream."[2]

A story without words had sown the seeds of hope in Rouland's world, but one sentence had shattered Olga's world. No one who hears a sentence like that will ever be the same. They might come back to life to some extent, but their lives will never be the same because their soul is aching. They taste things as though for the first time, but they taste different now. They rediscover the pleasure of music, but it is a different pleasure. It is sharper and more intense because they almost lost it.

They experience a desperate pleasure. Olga was eighteen at the time and a student in Toulouse. She had not a minute to spare, what with her work, her skiing trips to Praloup and the nights she spent dancing in Bandol. All that suddenly came to an end when the car hit a wall after failing to take a corner. If you become paraplegic at the age of eighteen, you are dead. At first, you are completely dead, and then life returns, but only to some extent, and it has a strange taste. Time no longer looks the same. You used to let the days go by. You either made good use of them or got bored. You perceived time as a slow sequence leading to a distant death that was certain but not quite real. When her accident shattered her soul, Olga came back to life with the curious feeling that she was living between two deaths. Part of her life had been killed inside her. Another part of it was waiting for the second death that would come later. People who are overcoming a trauma often have the strange feeling that time has been suspended. It fills them with despair when they think of the life they have lost, but it also heightens the pleasure of the life they can still enjoy. Olga could no longer go skiing or dancing, but she could study, think, talk, smile and weep a lot. She is now a brilliant geneticist who has a job and friends, and still does sport . . . in a wheelchair. 'As soon as I see someone with a spinal-cord injury, I know he will pull through if I can see a zest for life in his eyes. The ones who give the impression that they were injured just yesterday get bedsores. Let me tell you that bedsores are not just a skin problem. They are a necrosis. When you have bedsores, something dies inside you. Those who suffer but come to terms with their new life are better off. They do sport, even though they never used to. They make contacts, and they work harder.'[3]

A few years ago, people with spinal-cord injuries were patched up as well as they could be, and then put in institutions where, sadly, they were barely alive. The way society sees them is now changing; regardless of whether or not the wound is curable, patients are asked to use their abilities in order to learn to live their lives differently. It is the emotional and social context that gives them the few tutors in resilience who can help them to recover.

Olga's story allows us to situate the idea of resilience. A few decades ago, people with injuries like this were regarded as inferior beings. As only their physical injuries were taken into consideration, they were prevented from starting a new psychical life. In social terms, they all died. It took a long technological and cultural battle for most of them to succeed in coming back to life. But they were never the same.

Love, Despite It All

For Rouland, my polite play-acting had been a revelation: so it was possible not to despise his mother. Throughout his childhood, he had loved a woman everyone looked down upon. When his mother took him out of the boarding school where he had spent his earliest years, he had been happy living with this lively, warm woman. He was often bored because she slept all day and went out to work at night. The boy thought her job was something to do with the theatre. The way his school friends whispered and then burst out laughing soon taught him that she was not exactly an actress. That made Rouland sad, but he remained loyal to his mother and defended her reputation, sometimes with his fists.

The traumatic wound was inflicted day by day, but it was silent and almost invisible: the lecherous look in a friend's eye, the whispering that suddenly stopped as Rouland came near. Something half-spoken and almost unseen overwhelmed the little boy who was walled up alive in a world of mockery. I'd acted a part when I met his mother. I had only a vague memory of this, but it had been a point of reference for him. Without realizing it, I had tied the first knot in his growing resilience. From that day onwards, he had begun to hope again. He had quietly met two or three friends and had invited the bruisers from the rugby team home for tea. All the youngsters had been well behaved, and Rouland slowly learned to talk.

When he met his wife, he was still undergoing repairs and had to force himself to introduce her to his mother. The young woman was polite, and perhaps more than polite. Rouland did not want his mother and his girlfriend to see too much of one another because he loved the two women in different ways. After a few years of emotional training, he was surprised to find that he was no longer embarrassed when they met.

It was only because he had learned to hope again a few years earlier that he dared to embark on the adventure of a relationship, but it was his wife's emotional style that introduced him to a new way of loving. He was no longer walled up with a woman he loved even though he could not tell her that he loved her. My ceremonious scenario had triggered his hopes, but it was his first love who gave him confidence and transformed his silent suffering.

Her numbness had protected Olga from feeling any pain after her accident. She said that her body felt alien to her and that she could not understand what had happened. Everyone told her how brave she was being, but she was under anaesthetic. The pain started with a single sentence, when the doctor said: 'You might never walk again.' She had a vision of herself being unable to move, and that image turned her projects and even her past topsy-turvy. 'I should have had more good times . . . What does the future hold?' Until recently, our culture did not think about disability in terms of resilience, and Olga would have been cut in two, with one half of her dead and the other half dying. Now that we have begun to give the victims of spinal-cord injuries a better quality of care, the dead part is still subject to technological and medical imperatives, but the living part is not left to die. Olga came back to life, but her life was never the same. She had to prioritize skills that had been secondary before she had her accident. She invested a lot of herself in intellectual activities and improved her relational skills. She is now one of those people who sing the praises of weakness,[4] and who have grown strong in spite of their disabilities. She works in a laboratory and recently became pregnant. But the husband she met has had to adapt his way of loving to this special woman. And when their baby is born, he or she will have to become attached to parents who are not like other parents and who will pass on a very special inheritance.

Investment in hidden talents, defiance of the social gaze, and the adaptation of emotional styles: these are the themes of this book. When we become old enough to embark on a relationship, we present a self-image of what we would like to be, but we commit ourselves to the relationship with what we are, with our emotional style and with our past history. All couples sign special undertakings that give their relationship a personality of its own, which is strange, as we are talking about a combination of two different individuals. Their children will be born into the emotional field they have created, and it is there that they will have to grow up.

I speak of love because it is difficult to have a relationship without affecting one another and without transmitting an imprint of that love to our children. And I speak of a precipice because people who are in love with each other are standing on the edge of an abyss and are trying to walk away from it.

Bedsores serve as a metaphor for the sores on the souls of those who have suffered a mental trauma. 'Auschwitz is like a sore. And that's where I come from . . .' The psyche can die as the result of a psychotrauma. The inner world of the Auschwitz victims was pulverized and numbed with pain, and it could not give a shape to what the deportees perceived. Because they were being inundated with meaningless information, they were incapable of thinking. They did not know where they were and could not relate to others or to their own past. They were mutilated by life, yet their development was governed by a confluence of pressures: the severity of their injuries and the time it took for them to heal, the identity they constructed before the traumatic event, and the meaning they gave to their collapse. The psychical development of the deportees was influenced as much by their inner history as by what their families and their society said to them about their condition: 'It's terrible, you've had it and you'll never be able to get over it . . .' or 'You brought it on yourself really. How did you get yourself into that mess?' Victims are always guilty to some extent, aren't they?

The return to life occurs in secret, and it is accompanied by the strange pleasure that comes from the feeling of living on borrowed time. The trauma shatters the subject's previous personality and, when no one picks up the pieces so as to contain them, the subject either remains dead or has difficulty in coming back to life. But if the subject has the day-to-day emotional support of those around him or her, and if cultural discourse gives his wound a meaning, the subject can begin a different kind of development. 'Anyone who has suffered a trauma is forced to change.' If they do not, they stay dead.

Freud evokes the possibility of what we now call 'resilience' and takes the view that, given the extraordinary synthetic activity of the ego, it is scarcely possible to talk of trauma without also discussing the scars that develop afterwards.

We really have to ask ourselves why some people are irritated by the possibility of coming back to life.

As early as 1946, René Spitz studied the damage caused by emotional deprivation. The depression can be so great as to become anaclitic,[6] and the loss of emotional support can lead the child to abandon life, to let itself die because it has no one to live for. In 1958, the same psychoanalyst studied how depressed children can begin to develop once more. He found that, as they emerged from their anaclitic depression, their drives 're-fused' to some extent. They quickly became active again, and then became lively, cheerful and aggressive. In her preface to his *The First Year of Life*, Anna Freud remarked that it justified the hopes of those who wanted to study the problem in greater depth.[7] She was sharply criticized.[8] John Bowlby, the President of the British Psychoanalytic Society, also studied maternal deprivation. The initial inspiration for his work on attachment came from animal ethology. Bowlby defended the idea that the real world shapes the inner world of children.[9] His work was criticized by those who held that psychotraumas do not occur in the real world and believed that children were traumatized by 'the emergence of an unacceptable representation',[10] which can also be true. That is why, towards the end of his life, Bowlby reconciled everyone by demonstrating that the path an individual follows as he becomes resilient in the face of stressful events is strongly influenced by the attachment-schema he acquired in the first years of life.[11]

The Stories That Are Told Around the Wounded Can Make Things Better, or Worse

Freud thought that the seeds of adult suffering were sown during childhood. We now have to add that the way families and the cultural environment talk about wounds can either attenuate or exacerbate that suffering, depending upon what stories they tell.

Almost all the child-soldiers of Latin America, Africa and the Near East have been traumatized. Those who succeed in coming back to life are forced to leave their villages, and sometimes even their countries, in order to 'start again from scratch' and to avoid the shameful label they have been given because of their histories. Many child-soldiers are afraid of peace because war is all they have ever known. But some of them want to escape that fate and ask to go to school far away from the places where they were soldiers. They can change, provided that the social organization allows them to do so. When they are asked what they would have become if they had not experienced the ravages of war, they say, 'I would have done what my dad did,' which is only natural given that, in peacetime, adult attachment figures provide the models with which children identify. Because they were actors in a war, children who have learned to eroticize violence become mercenaries. In any modern war, between 10 and 15 per cent of fighters will discover the delights that horror can procure. Women, who are increasingly involved in military action, as in Colombia, the Middle East and Sri Lanka, experience the same terrifying pleasure. The number of trauma victims varies, depending on the conditions in which the war is waged, but the average is an estimated 30 per cent for the first year. Most children are neither depressed nor excited by the violence, but they are usually demoralized and in despair.

Many child-soldiers dream of becoming doctors 'to save lives', or writers 'in order to bear witness'. But the social context is such that it is not always possible for them to undertake that long journey. Those who do succeed in having a family or in becoming doctors or journalists will never forget the trauma they have suffered. On the contrary, they will make use of it to determine their vocations. They will never know the serene happiness that a real family living in a culture of peace would have given them, but they may succeed in coming back to the land of the living if they can snatch a few minutes of peace and give the chaos they have experienced a meaning that makes it bearable.

The best way to torture human beings is to reduce them to despair by telling them: '*Hier ist kein warum*' ('There is no why here').[12] That phrase hurls them into the world of things, subordinates them to things and actually turns them into things. We have to work at giving things a meaning if we are to be able to offer a helping hand to someone whose psyche is dying and to help them to find their place in the human world once more. In that world, there is a why: 'The ability to translate the images they have seen and the commotions they have experienced into words and verbal presentations that can be shared, so as to give them a meaning that can be communicated'[13] restores their humanity. A love for 'whys' is a precious factor in developing resilience and it makes it possible to re-tie the first knots in the bond that has been torn apart.

Germaine Tillion, a social anthropologist with a special interest in the Maghreb, was deported to Ravensbrück in 1943 because of her involvement in the Resistance. As soon as she got there she began to use her observational skills, which had been honed by her contacts with the Berbers of the Aurès mountains. She tried to understand how the camp functioned and she would give talks in her hut at night, explaining how the guards wanted to work the prisoners to death.

Geneviève de Gaulle-Anthonioz, niece of General de Gaulle and deported for her Resistance activities, told her: 'When we listened to you, we were no longer *Stück* [pieces] but people and we could fight because we could understand.'[14]

To which Germaine Tillion replied: 'The ability to interpret phenomena around us gave us moral support, made us less afraid [. . .] as soon as I got home, I devoted myself to researching our deportation.'[15]

If we are not willing to let our humanity be destroyed, we have to look for the hidden meanings and invisible structures that allow this absurdly cruel system to function. The fact of being fascinated with the torturers sometimes results in an identification with the aggressor, but the attention the victims pay them usually imprints a memory which subsequently allows a metamorphosis. Such memories create a space for inner freedom: 'They can't take that away from me, they can't stop me from understanding it and using it as soon as I get a chance.' If we can construct a meaning, we can develop a feeling of belonging and protect our identities by containing them inside a group that uses the same words and images, and that respects the rites that weave solidarity. As soon as they were liberated, both women committed themselves to the struggle against torture in Algeria and to the fight against world hunger.

'We now know that reconnecting things and giving them a meaning after the event [. . .] does trauma-victims good,'[16] but the way they judge events is always influenced by the sores that are still there in their stories.

Working on meaning is the most private of activities. Anything that has been imprinted with a trauma will always fuel representations of the memories that constitute our inner identity. That meaning lives on inside us and provides our life with its themes.

II

Resilience as Anti-Destiny

'It's funny how things take on a meaning once they're over . . . that's when the story begins.'[1]

We talk and talk. One word comes after another, but it is only when the music of the voice tells us that the full stop is coming that we finally understand where the words are leading us. We get on with our lives and facts pile up, but it is only when time allows us to look back at ourselves that we understand where our lives were leading. 'It is only because the words succeed one another and then die that their meaning can emerge.'[2] When our childhood is coming to an end, we turn it into a narrative, and when our lives are coming to an end, we discover why we had to live them.

It is time that makes us aware of meaning. I should say: it is my representation of time, the way I remember my past in order to organize my memories and to enjoy the daydreams that imbue what I perceive with meaning. The stories I tell myself about what has happened to me and the pictures I paint of the happiness I had hoped for introduce into me a world that is not there and that is not present, but I still experience it with great intensity.

The Humiliating Omelette

A humiliating omelette and a disturbing cup of tea allowed me to understand that the meaning of our lives derives from events that are no longer in context.

Thérèse thought that the life she was living was a little too quiet but she could not bring herself to say that it was dull. The high point of her day was doing her shopping at the supermarket at about eleven every morning. That day, her trolley bumped into that of a young man, as happens so often. His comments transformed the incident and made her smile. A little later, he helped her to put her shopping into the car. A little later, he waved to her as he drove out of the car park. A little later, he parked in her street just as she got home. A little later, she was astounded to find herself in bed with a charming man she had only met two hours ago.[3]

Afterwards, Thérèse could not get over what had happened. She said to him: 'It's midday. I'll make an omelette if you like.' He said that was a good idea and that while she cooked it he would go and check why his car was making odd noises. When she heard the engine start up, she felt funny, went to the window and saw the car disappearing at top speed around the corner at the end of the street. She felt as though she had been punched in the face and burst into tears. She felt humiliated.

Suppose her transient lover had shared Thérèse's omelette. Her sexual adventure would have taken on a whole different meaning: 'It was a moment of madness, but it was nice. Not like me at all. What came over me? Don't think about it. Yes, do think about it and think of it as something that livened up a dull day.'

It was the way he ran away that gave a meaning to the encounter that had taken place a few minutes earlier. Thérèse was furious as she stood there with the plate in her hand. She did not eat the omelette, which symbolized 'humiliation', whereas the same omelette could have meant 'naughty but nice' if her lover had shared it with her. The way events had unfolded had transformed a thing into a sign.

A shocked Thérèse replayed certain scenes and recalled a few phrases. Even though she was resentful, she did feel the curious pleasure that comes from satisfying a need. She rewrote certain scenes and imagined what she should have said. 'I should have told him . . . should have realized . . . told him where to get off.' At the same time, she was reconstructing her past, integrating her adventure into the story of her life and trying to discover some analogy, some repetition or some consistency that would allow her to understand the way she organized her life. 'Men always let me down . . . it was the same with my first boyfriend.'

Now that she had found an orientation in her history, she could lay down a rule that made her feel more confident about her future: 'I can't go on like this. I have to learn not to rely on my own judgement because I put too much trust in men.' By trying to find a few painful episodes that had been repeated in her past life, Thérèse was once more consciously presenting ('re-presenting') a scenario that was inscribed in her memory, and reworking it. Although she had been hurt, she was not in fact brooding over what had happened but trying, on the contrary, to find a new direction for the future. This sad task of remembering made her feel secure because it helped her to establish a rule that would allow her to be in better control of her life in future. Now that it had been integrated into a story about her, the signifying omelette could allow her to discover how her life was oriented.

Our tendency to tell ourselves stories about what has happened to us is a resilience factor, provided that we can give a meaning to what has happened and rework it in emotional terms.

Thérèse was obviously not responding to the eggs; she was responding to the meaning that had been given to the omelette by the way things had turned out. Thérèse had not been humiliated by the omelette itself, but she was mortified by the meaning she had given it because of the context in which it was prepared and her own past history.

Human beings could not live in a world without memories or dreams. If they were prisoners of the present, their world would be meaningless. This story about a cup of tea illustrates the point. You are quietly working in the garden and then go into the living room to cool down. You are surprised to find your children staring in horror at the television. On the screen, a man is just about to drink a cup of tea. You ask yourself what is so horrifying about that, and you cannot understand why they were alarmed because you were in the garden when, in the film, the hero's wife put cyanide in his tea.[4] Your children, on the other hand, remembered the scene and knew in advance that the man was going to die. They were experiencing the delicious horror of a detective film, whereas you were witnessing a banality that had no meaning. Their memory gave the cup of tea a meaning. They knew that the object was much more than just a cup of tea because it was the bringer of death. The present they were perceiving was imbued with the past, and that provoked a delicious anxiety about the future.

Even Public Words Have a Private Meaning

This ability to give things a meaning that has been imprinted on us in the course of our development can be readily observed in narration. In order to construct a story about ourselves that expresses our personal identity, we have to master time, remember a few images from the past that made an impression on us, and turn them into a story. But all the words that we exchange in the course of our everyday lives have been penetrated by the meaning they acquired in our past.

After an unbelievable childhood in the Poland of the 1940s, Maria Nowak developed a memory typical of those who have been traumatized: a mixture of clear recollections surrounded by vague memories. As a little girl, she saw her house being burned down, endured air raids and suffered the loss of her father, the arrest of her sister and the constant fear that she herself would be imprisoned. She was there when the horse came back to its stable, carrying the corpse of her friend who had been shot in the forehead. She was moved to pity by the beauty of corpses covered with a delicate blanket of snow. Eventually, starving and abandoned, she was placed in orphanages and foster families. She was guaranteed material protection there, but she met no one who could help her to nurture a little emotionality. When Poland was 'liberated' by the Russians, her mother found her and asked her what had happened during the two years they had been separated. The little girl recalled: 'Nothing special. And it was true. I was living in a world where there was no time, life or tenderness. I survived but I'm exhausted. That's all." Maria had been better protected in the orphanages than she would have been if she had remained alone on the streets. However, the emotional desert in which she had been living could not arouse any of the inner emotional stirrings that might have sensitized her or constructed an image, a temporal marker or a signpost that she could use to construct a story about herself: 'No time . . . and no tenderness.' No image to commit to memory.

The fact that her circumstances meant that she could recollect no images and no words certainly does not mean that she had no memory. But it was a memory without memories. As a little girl, she had been preferentially sensitized to certain events and now gave them specific meaning. Later on, when she became a student in Paris, a nice young man invited Maria out to dinner. Before they went into the restaurant, he asked, 'Are you hungry?' She replied: 'No, I'm all right now, I eat every day.'[6]

Convention has it that words are the same for all those who speak the same language, but they take on particular meanings that derive from the private history of each individual speaker. If we are to have a representation of time past and future, our emotional relationships must highlight certain objects, gestures and words and turn them into events. That is how we construct the internal apparatus that gives a meaning to the world we perceive.

This is why we have to wait for the end of the sentence and for the end of our lives for the meaning to appear. So long as there is no full stop at the end of a sentence or a life, it is always possible to rework their meanings.

A Cathedral Inside the Head

Meaning dawns at the same time as life – animal or human – but it is constructed in different ways in different species, and depends upon the development and history of the individual concerned.

An animal understands the real world in which it lives. It responds to it with goal-adjusted behaviour. It perceives the animal objects its nervous system abstracts from its environment. Biological memory processes appear at a very early stage, even in very simple organisms. Once the tens of thousands of neurons which, in spiders for example, constitute a small 'cerebral' ganglion have been wired up, any living creature becomes capable of remembering. It can therefore learn to solve the various problems created by changing ecological environments and can develop in a number of different ways. Once its nervous system can retrieve the data it perceived in the past and respond to it, we can speak of sensory representation. That memory ascribes an emotion to the objects it perceives, and that emotion triggers attraction or flight, depending upon how it learned to process information in the past.[7]

A human infant can also understand the real world. During the last weeks of pregnancy, the foetus responds to the elementary sense-data (noises, mechanical shocks, the taste of the amniotic fluid, its mother's emotions) with which it is becoming familiar. This explains why, as soon as it is born, its world is structured by particularly significant objects: it perceives them more easily than other objects.

Every living creature has, however, a small degree of biological freedom, as it can respond either by running away or by surrendering, by being aggressive or placatory. It is only when representations of images or words appear that the subject can begin to rework the meanings imprinted on its memory. Evolution has given us a natural capacity for resilience.

The birth of speech brings about the death of things. Initially, things were victorious and forced themselves on our memory but, once we are able to create symbols and use one object to represent another, our inner world can replace things with thoughts.

In order to illustrate the extent to which we inhabit this new world, I have often related the following fable, which I have always attributed to Charles Péguy.[8] On his way to Chartres, Péguy saw a man breaking stones with a big sledgehammer by the side of the road. His face was a picture of misery and his gestures were full of anger. Péguy stopped and asked: 'What are you doing, monsieur?' 'You can see what I'm doing,' the man replied, 'this stupid, painful job is all I could find.' A little further on, Péguy saw another man. He was breaking rocks too, but his face was calm and his gestures were harmonious. 'What are you doing, monsieur?' asked Péguy. 'Oh, I'm making a living. It's hard work, but at least I'm out of doors.' Further on, a third stonebreaker radiated happiness. He smiled as he put down his hammer and looked at the fragments of stones with pleasure. 'What are you doing?' asked Péguy. 'Building a cathedral!'

A stone devoid of meaning subjected the wretched man to an unmediated reality in which he understood nothing but the weight of the sledgehammer and his immediate suffering. In contrast, the man with a cathedral inside his head had transfigured the stones, and was already enjoying the exultantly beautiful image of the cathedral of which he was so proud. But the inner world of the stonebreakers conceals a mystery: why do some of them have a cathedral inside their heads, when others see nothing but stones?

Were it not for our memories and our hopes, we would be living in a world in which there was no reason. In order to make the prison of the present tolerable, we fill it with immediate pleasures. This behavioural adaptation apparently gives us a facile pleasure, but instant pleasures lead to acrimony because perpetual pleasure is impossible. If the pleasure lasts too long, we become indifferent to it, and the slightest frustration leads to bitterness and aggressiveness.[9] A life devoted to pleasure plunges us into despair just as surely as a life without pleasure.

Meaning Does Not Have Time to Be Born in the Soul of Minute-Man

'We experience reality only through the meaning we ascribe to it; not as a thing in itself, but as something interpreted.'[10] Our technological victories have resulted in the recent invention of minute-man.[11] People who are in a hurry like doing things in a rush because it forces them to act without having to think, but they have become convicts whose lifestyle is organized around their relationship with time: 'We are completely free to enjoy ourselves. Friends and Epicureans, let us band together to fight the killjoys who want to stop us from doing just that.' Such solidarity allows us to experience the joys of outraged virtue: 'We're not doing any harm. We just want to enjoy life.' But, as this reflex does not let time last long enough to give birth to reason, these pleasure-centred groups break up very quickly and transmit nothing to their friends and children. In contrast, the four hundred years it takes to build a cathedral make us happy even though the cathedral does not exist yet. Meaning gives us a lasting happiness that we can pass on, whereas solitary pleasures are momentary. But a combination of pleasure and meaning makes it worthwhile to spend our lives breaking stones.

We construct meanings inside our heads, using what was there before us and with what will be there when we are gone: history and daydreams, our ancestors and our descendants. If, however, our culture or our circumstances do not provide us with a few emotional ties that can move us and construct memories, then the lack of emotion and the loss of meaning turn us into minute-men. We can enjoy the pleasures of the moment but, in times of trouble, we will not have the building blocks of resilience.

This is another way of saying that certain families, certain groups and certain cultures facilitate resilience, whereas others block it. It so happens that recent work by the World Health Organization confirms this idea by establishing a link between the objective improvement of conditions of existence and the disintegration of families and groups. Professor Norman Sartorius's findings show that, as a society becomes more organized, individuals become dissociated from one another.[12]

As their conditions of existence improve, human beings need each other less and less. Indeed, looking after others distracts us from the pursuit of self-improvement. In a society where no one can survive on their own, in contrast, looking after others is a form of self-protection.

Rejecting the progress which has transformed the human condition within the space of fifty years is out of the question, but we have to remember that progress always has its side effects. Improved individual performances lead to the dissolution of bonds with others and increase our vulnerability to trauma. Everything is fine if we are still in the race but if anything goes wrong, life becomes too harsh. It is difficult to stitch up traumatic wounds when life is emotionless and meaningless.

This phenomenon was highlighted in surveys about young people's life projects carried out immediately after the end of the Second World War and at the start of the technological explosion. In the defeated country of Austria, 40 per cent of young people were drifting aimlessly, but in the victorious America, 80 per cent of young people said that their lives had no meaning.[13] There was a lot of talk of an existential void: young people filled it by chasing after immediate pleasures or by giving their lives an ersatz meaning by joining extremist sects or communities.

If we are to construct meaning, we must have a

common project. But if it is to give rise to a representation that makes us feel happy, that project must be long term and diversified. When a culture's project is restricted to immediate well-being there is not enough time for meaning to be born in the souls of the subjects who live in that society. Conversely, when a culture's only proposal for the future is a perfect society that will exist in a different place and time – it is always somewhere else – it sacrifices the pleasures of life and concentrates solely on the ecstasies to come. Utopias kill the real in order to exaggerate the happiness of a radiant future. It is always jam tomorrow.

The Story of a Very Meaningful Vase

Given that we are all capable of representation, we cannot stop ourselves ascribing a meaning to the events that punctuate our histories and contribute to our identities. We can give an ordeal a meaning: 'With hindsight, I am proud that I did not let myself be beaten.' We can also transfigure a failure: 'My mother was a cleaner and she always told me: "You're going to be a surgeon even though you don't want to, so that I can be proud of you . . ." I was very worried about sitting my exams but when I failed them, I discovered that she didn't die as a result. My anxiety vanished and after that I allowed myself to do what I liked.' We can even change the meaning of an object whose circulation 'tells' us something about our inner history.

No one could say that Sabine was happy in her foster family. She wasn't unhappy either. She was in much the same position as a foreigner who is living in a mediocre hotel with people whose language she can hardly understand. She was waiting for better times, and she paid the price for her future autonomy by being abnormally well behaved. One day, she gave her foster mother a heavy, expensive vase for her birthday. All she put in it were a few sprigs of lilac she had picked on a nearby building site. Her foster mother was annoyed because the flowers looked so cheap and lost her temper: 'After all I've done for you!' She threw away the flowers and kept the vase. Sabine thought to herself: 'Even the language of flowers leads to misunderstandings between us.'

Sabine became a police officer. A few years later, she was explaining to a probationer that a banal object can be used as a murder weapon when she was called to the hospital: 'Someone in the family'. The probationer went with her in the car. She found that her foster mother's husband had just been operated on for a sub-dural haematoma. This is a blood clot on the meninges, which are between the skull and the brain, and can be caused by a brain trauma. As Sabine was leaving the treatment room, her foster mother came up to her, handed her a bag and said: 'My husband almost died because of you.' Sabine opened the bag and saw . . . the vase! Her foster mother added: 'We still fight . . . I threw your vase at his head.' The probationer looked at his feet. Sabine picked up the vase, broke it and threw the pieces into the gutter. The probationer smiled.

Objects take on a meaning because our memory establishes links between things and makes them coherent. In a meaningless world, we would see nothing but fragments of the real world and would respond only to stimuli that existed in the present: it's great or it's terrible, it attracts me or repels me, I like it or I don't like it. The world would be seen in a fragmentary way because it would be fragmentary, because there would be no thread to hold the fragments together, and because the world would have no soul. But given that we belong to a species that is capable of processing information – past or future – outside any context and because we can respond to it emotionally, behaviourally and verbally, we can free ourselves from the tyranny of things and submit to the representations we have created.

As a child, Sabine spent all her savings on this expensive vase because it was her way of saying that she was a nice girl and would try to be no trouble to her foster family. As always, her foster mother failed to understand the meaning of things. Because she was annoyed about how pathetic the flowers were, she thought that, by giving her the vase, Sabine had – intentionally or otherwise – given her a murder weapon. When Sabine broke the vase and threw the pieces into the gutter, she felt both sad and relieved. But it was only when the sequence of events came to an end that the object's meaning emerged: 'I nearly killed my husband because of your vase (because of you).'

This example demonstrates that a traumatized subject can be so overwhelmed and submerged by information that he or she cannot respond to a confusing world. Senseless violence means that death is never far away. Molehills look like mountains and the world loses its clarity. How are we to behave in such a world?

Narrative as Fog-Lamp

So long as the trauma has no meaning, we are shattered, stupefied and confused by a whirlwind of contradictory information that leaves us incapable of taking decisions. But, given that we are obliged to give a meaning to the phenomena and objects that 'speak' to us, we do have a way of clearing the fog that comes rolling in when we experience a psychotrauma – and that is by means of narrative.

In this case, narration becomes a way of working

on meaning. Not all histories, however, can be socialized, and they have to be adapted to suit other people,
who find it difficult to listen to them. The event is
metamorphosed into a narrative by doing two things:
we externalize events and we situate them in time.
The listener has to be there, but must remain silent.
Sometimes the witness exists only in the imagination
of the injured subject, who is talking to a virtual
listener as he tells himself his story. For those whose
souls have been damaged, narration is an act that gives
them the feeling that 'the events seem to be recounting
themselves'.[14] Memories of images pass through their
minds, and they are framed by words that comment
on them, explain them, hesitate and then begin to
describe the scene by using other expressions. Thanks
to this work, the narrative can slowly extract the event
from the self. The narrative exposition locates
significant events that found their way into our minds
in the past. 'That is the only way that the past, the
absent and the dead can return to the present world
of the living, to the stage of the text and the image,
to the stage of the representation. It is only then that
they can become re-presentations.'[15]

It is only between the ages of seven and ten that
we acquire the ability to construct a discourse that
allows us to master our inner worlds. Until we reach
that age, we are prisoners of the context, in the same
way that children burst into laughter when their eyes

are still filled with tears or are reduced to despair by a minor disappointment, but experience great joy when they see a passing butterfly. Young children find it hard to answer the question, 'What did you do today?' because doing so requires a representation of time. Children can describe external events before they are able to construct an inner world for themselves.

Children aged between about seven and ten tend to talk about themselves by making a series of statements that attempt to answer the question, 'Who do others think I am?' Their discourse becomes sexualized at a very early age: 'I am a girl. My name is Sylvie. I have short blonde hair.' Girls often use the verb 'to love': 'I love Madeleine, I love my dress, I love the colour of my eyes.' Boys prefer 'to be' and 'to have': 'I'm tall. I'm good at football. I have a good bike.'

The younger the child, the more assertive the discourse. It is only with hindsight that nuances and doubts creep in. Girls attach more importance to the gaze of others, whilst boys increasingly speak in terms of hierarchical points of reference. Studies show that discourse becomes gendered at a very early age, but they cannot explain the origins of the difference.

The way we spontaneously rework our self-representation depending on our age, our gender and our emotional and cultural surroundings is testimony to how our self-image can be modified by the effects of all the stories we hear. Stories are more elaborate and less stereotypical than discourses, and they mean that facts have to be intentionally reorganized into memories before we can construct a self-representation that is addressed to those around us, to our culture and to a third party who can be either real or imaginary.

When the subject cannot undertake this task because he or she is too young, because his or her family silences him or her, or because the brain-damage caused by an accident or illness makes it impossible to represent time, resilience becomes difficult. But so long as our self-image can be modified, and so long as our involvement in psychical and social reality allows us to work on it, resilience is possible because it means, quite simply, that we can in a sense go on developing after our psychic death.

The Force of Destiny

Meaning is born of the hindsight that allows us to look back at ourselves and our past. This constraint explains why some people overestimate the resilience that offers them the beginnings of hope, whilst others submit to their misfortune as though it were their destiny. From their perspective, destiny must always win because it is tautological: 'He died because he had to die.' There is no answer to this argument because it is put forward as though it had a meaning and because the outcome is there in the prediction.[16] This unavoidable truth encourages tautologists to string their arguments together: 'So he studied medicine because, with parents like that, he had no option . . .', 'He married a strict woman because, as you can well imagine, with the unstable childhood he had . . .'. In the Middle Ages, the explanation for the tendency of bodies to fall was that they had a falling virtue. Nowadays, we say that he killed his wife because he had a death drive. This retrospective illusion gives believers in destiny a great feeling of coherence. When it is presented like a slogan, meaning has a tranquillizing effect and takes away the feeling of guilt: 'I had no choice . . . something deep inside me made me do it . . . It was written . . . It's not my fault.' Those who worship destiny celebrate the way we submit to the dark forces that rule us. In their view, the outcome explains the prediction: 'I told him that the trauma he thought was healed would reopen one day.' Fate appears to have complete control over us, like some diabolical power that lurks inside us, or like an enormous psychic parasite that is difficult to see and that controls us without our knowing it.

Cultures of certainty often ascribe cheap meanings to unexpected events: a rabbi in Jerusalem recently wrote: 'The Jews who died in Auschwitz must have committed terrible crimes for them to be so cruelly punished by God.' TV evangelists in America evoke 'the sins and licentiousness of New Yorkers' to explain the attacks of 11 September 2001. Enormous causes are the only possible explanations for such enormous effects. For those with a taste for extreme beliefs, any dogma that lays down the truth is acceptable. We are all – persecutors and the persecuted, victims and executioners – ruled by an inexorable force that can explain every tragedy.

People who have never been traumatized find this submission to destiny reassuring. It is a way of avoiding anxiety about uncertainty and it takes away the guilt of war criminals, who quite calmly say: 'I was just obeying orders.' In Rwanda, the girls who identified classmates so that they could be executed, or just have their arms cut off, now sigh: 'It wasn't me. I was possessed by the Devil.' Edith Uwanyiligara writes: 'While we were running away, we kept quiet, like people who had been humiliated. Wherever we went, we heard them saying: "There's some Tutsis; they smell bad . . . we have to kill them, get rid of them." Even little children at primary school . . . threw stones at us and shouted: "They're Tutsis; they're cockroaches."'[17] The genocide had reduced the survivors to such a sorry state that witnesses felt disgusted when they looked at them. They must have committed terrible crimes to end up in that state. The effect that explained the cause also justified mass murder.

Descriptions of the sores that are eating away at the souls of the traumatized are also affected by the ideological delusions of those who believe that a monster lurks in the hearts of damaged children, and that the devil will ride out one day or another. Children who have been abused become abusive parents in their turn. They fall in love with their aggressors and the demon inside makes them commit atrocities. The very fact of seeing a subject who has been attacked solely as a victim gives the impression that the partners involved in the violence were very close to one another. They are victims, so they must have been close to their aggressors. 'She's a victim, but she must have provoked him, she's partly to blame . . .' Victims are suspect; they have been initiated by their closeness to death. They were held in the arms of their assailants. We cannot trust them. Assailant and victim should be put in the same sack and thrown in the river, as they were in the Middle Ages. The feeling that some intimacy must have existed between the partners in violence triggers automatic arguments: any victim should be ashamed of the evil that has been implanted within her because 'the deplorable teachings of vice leave the seeds of corruption in the souls of its victims'.[18] Nineteenth-century courts provide an astonishing paraphrase of the beliefs of those who still think that evil lurks in the soul of damaged children and that, one day, the devil will come forth from them: victims are filthy!

The extreme beliefs implicit in these linear arguments are spelled out by those who believe in curses. They insist that a wound can be passed down through the generations, and say that secrets can trigger third-generation psychoses. Psychical wounds do indeed mean that the personality of the parent who envelops the child is organized in a particular way. It transmits a shadow that triggers disorders, but it can also be an invitation to the pleasure of solving puzzles.

Emotional Adaptation

Resilience is all about stitching up traumatic wounds. If, however, we are to think in terms of resilience, we have to turn our histories into a vision in which every encounter is an existential choice. This way of giving our lives a meaning that is not inexorable is testimony to our capacity for inner freedom. It allows thousands of possible scenarios, with all the hesitations, sudden changes and anxieties that are implicit in any choice. People who think in this way feel at ease in cultures of uncertainty, where they can easily 'venture' their lives.[19] This minor freedom is a craft industry in which every gesture and every word can modify the reality that carries us along and can construct resilience as an anti-destiny.

Finding a partner is certainly one of the major

choices we make in our lives. Anyone who has been hurt by life commits himself to his partner, but he also commits his past, his dreams and his way of giving things a meaning. His partner must also shape an image of his wound and of their hopes for the future. Both partners have to come to terms with each other's inner world, blossom, reassure one another, compromise, and sometimes fight. This joint emotional and historical effort creates a sensory bubble for any children they may have. It creates an envelope of gestures, crying, laughter, mimicry and words that will shape their children's early development until such time as they are old enough to have a sexual relationship.

- How do wounded souls meet?
- Does a couple's contract heighten their resilience or drive them further apart?
- What do resilient parents transmit to the children they give birth to?

These are the questions we will be looking at.

III

When a Meeting Is a Reunion

Perfection and the Worm

Could interminable adolescence be a sign of healthy development?

Whether or not children feel good about themselves depends upon how their environment tutors their development. There comes a day when, all at once, the world arouses previously unknown emotions. The child knew that little girls are not little boys, that women are not men and that mums are not quite women. But over the last few months, those sexual notions have acquired different emotional connotations. Women's bodies suddenly arouse new emotions in adolescent boys, and those emotions are at once pleasurable and a source of anxiety. Girls look at boys in a new way, and hope to attract the attention of the youngsters they were laughing at only a few weeks ago.

These new emotions and this intense feeling of being attracted to the opposite sex can be attributed to the secretion of the sexual hormones that make pubescent young people hypersensitive to a kind of information that, until very recently, meant nothing to them. Biological changes announce puberty but they do not explain adolescence. A boy suddenly feels a strange partiality for a girl's body, and has to use all his relational skills, all the emotional style that is currently at his disposal and the whole manner of loving that he has already acquired in order to approach her. He wants to get close to her but is still uncertain as to how to go about doing so. Adolescence is not necessarily a time of crisis, but it always marks a change of emotional orientation.

A young person who feels drawn towards the opposite sex and wants to have a particular kind of relationship cannot avoid the question: 'Will he (she) have me?' This calls into question the mental self-representation that young person has constructed in the course of his or her childhood. It could be an image-representation: 'With a body like mine, no man could want me.' Or it could be a verbal representation: 'Given my history of child abuse, he (she) will definitely reject me.'

We are waiting for our first love, and our image of the other has already been shaped by the internal self-image we have constructed: 'Women are angels and I'm overawed by them. How can you expect anyone as perfect as that to fall in love with a worm like me?' It is also possible to think: 'Girls are vulnerable little things and I can use them just as I like because I am stronger and bolder than they are.' As we prepare to commit ourselves to someone we love, the self-representation we acquired as children always comes into play. We use our memories of the past to prepare ourselves for this new commitment: 'Who are my parents? Was I good at school? Do I have a gift for friendship? Am I sad? Am I brainy?' Our self-image is the capital we invest when we make the most risky choices we will ever make in our lives: those affecting our love and our social lives.

This self-representation becomes a belief that determines our commitments: 'I was no good at school, I'm thick, so I'll have to choose a job for thickies.' A boy who thinks like this is preparing his bitterness and is already constructing what he imagines himself, his past and his future to be. So much so that an adolescent who recalls a history of repeated emotional losses will tend to fear the future love he so desperately desires. He dreams of a girl who will give him emotional security, whatever the cost. Similarly, a girl who has had a wretched childhood, and who has suffered as a result, will take refuge in the violent hope of doing whatever she has to do in order to ensure that she will never go hungry again. Adolescence is therefore a turning point. It is a moment in our lives when our commitments depend upon our self-image. It is a sensitive period,[1] when we invest, with varying degrees of success, the intellectual, historical and emotional capital we accumulated as we grew up. We also gamble on the future, and on our ability to rework our self-image, which depends upon the people and the environments we encounter at this point in time.

Adolescence: Dangerous Bend

'Sensitive period' is not synonymous with 'pathological period'. Fewer than 2 per cent of children suffer from depression, even when they live in difficult conditions. A little boy whose parents are poor or ill can still escape his environment thanks to moments of friendship, games of football or something he has learned at school, and that is enough to make him happy. An adolescent must rework his attachment and break free from the parental bond in order to commit himself to another relationship that is both emotional and sexual. This means taking a big risk, even in a normal situation, as he must leave his secure base if he wishes to evolve and pursue his development. The incidence of depression then rises to 10 per cent. Non-pathological adolescents (90 per cent) are not necessarily easy to live with either. The intensity of their emotions and the vehemence with which they express them affect their parents and lead to fights in 30 to 40 per cent of cases.[2] Adolescence is a sensitive period but not a period of distress. The emotional relationship can change if the environment allows the emotions to calm down and lets the adolescent commit him- or herself to a life-project.

For adolescents, rows at home are no obstacle to attachment. The hyperexpressivity typical of this age group explains the apparent contradiction between the surveys that reveal that over 80 per cent of adolescents love their parents even though 50 per cent of families experience conflict. A securely attached parent does not exacerbate the conflict, but calms the adolescent down and waits for him to express affection once more. But when a parent has, because of her own history, invested too much in her child, she is wounded by this vehemence and feels that she is not equipped for her parental role: 'I gave up a career I loved so that you would not have to change schools. And look what I get in return!' And a banal conflict turns into a painful relationship.

The way emotions are reworked during the sensitive period of adolescence is gender specific. The other day, I took the little boat that shuttles backwards and forwards between Toulon and Les Sablettes. I was surrounded by a gang of very lively girls and boys. 'I'll keep an eye on the thirteen-year-olds,' said one of the accompanying adults. The girls were twice the size of the boys. They looked like sexual delicacies and were doing all they could to assert their emergent femininity: low-cut tops, studded belly-buttons, and very mini miniskirts. Everything that could be sexualized was highlighted: nails, eyes, lips, hair. For the girls concerned, this was not so much a sexual invitation as a proud assertion of the advantages of being a woman. The boys looked frail alongside these big girls. They were smooth-faced, smooth-skinned sweeties who allowed themselves to be mothered by the big girls who put their arms around them and laughed at their stupidity when the little boys suddenly began to punch them in the stomach. The girls took up clumsy and pointless combat stances, and then reverted to being just friends with the boys. An adolescent girl who mixes with boys who are just beginning their metamorphosis has already been pubescent for two to three years. That is a huge difference at an age when physical and intellectual maturation plays an important role in social orientation. And yet, at the same time we see a reversal of moods. Within a few months, boys who were a bit down in the mouth and dominated by the girls become cheerful and assertive, sometimes too much so. In contrast, girls, who were less prone to depression than boys until they reached puberty, become fearful, less self-confident and much more anxious. They often seek the approval of adults, which makes it easier for them to adapt to any form of culture.[3] This is another way of saying that the same situation can have different psychological impacts, depending on the age and gender of the receptor. Boys, who are more vulnerable when their parents divorce, find identification difficult if they have no father and seek out situations in which risk-taking acts as an initiatory ordeal. Girls, who are more advanced in both physical and intellectual terms, find divorce easier but feel that their style is being cramped if they live alone with their mothers. These adolescent girls sometimes believe that they will find their autonomy by becoming mothers at a very early age. One in two sixteen-year-old girls in Québec has already had sexual relations (as compared with one in four boys) and 5 per cent of these very young women will fall pregnant.[4]

Involvement in a sexual relationship is therefore governed by convergent forces: age, biological maturation, which differs in accordance with gender, the family and cultural context at the time the young person meets a partner, as well as his or her history and self-image prior to the sexual act. A boy from a poor background and living in a restricted space will tend not to attribute much importance to school and will choose a manual job if the social context offers him one. But a girl who feels that her style is being cramped by a mother who is poor and on her own will compensate for her educational and relational failures by becoming pregnant at an early age. This collection of biological, historical, familial and cultural data describes a population of adolescents who develop without experiencing any psychotraumas but who do go through some severe ordeals. Traumatized adolescents are subject to the same convergent forces, but in their case their personalities have already been torn apart.

This type of argument, which integrates data from different sources, is very different from the linear arguments in which a single cause has a single effect. When we do not feel well, we want to think in linear terms because we hope that a single cause will provide a solution. Such mistaken explanations provide us with a momentary relief because they shed light on a partial truth, but they blind us to the other reasons that make us feel ill. No single cause provides a complete explanation.

The World Tastes As We Expect It to Taste

When a damaged child reaches adolescence, he begins the inevitable emotional reworking that is triggered by his hormonal surges and the prohibition on incest, which gives the world a particular flavour. The damage inflicted on him as a child has made him preferentially sensitive to one type of information. Children who have grown up in a country that is at war are better than others at perceiving the sound of a car door being slammed or of a car backfiring. They respond to these significant noises by diving under a table and then re-emerging without feeling that they are being ridiculous because, in their minds, this is simply survival behaviour. The fact of having grown up in a country at war has taught them to have a preferential perception of a type of sonic information that is of significance only to them. That signifier has been inscribed in their memories and will trigger the same response in a country that is at peace, and where diving under the table makes people want to laugh because such behaviour is no longer adapted to the situation.

This behaviour, which has often been observed, allows us to understand that our responses to an immediate stimulus can be explained in the light of our past experiences.[5] A new-born baby responds to the parameters that exist in its real environment[6] but, once it is five months old, it responds to the Internal Working Models that have been constructed in its young memory. A baby learns at a very early age to extract from the environment a preferential form constructed, at this stage, by the mother's sense-perception of her environment. Once that form has been inscribed in its memory, it imbues the child with a feeling of self. If a mother mistreats her baby or handles it roughly, the child will learn to have a heightened perception of the sounds and gestures that announce the brutal act. The child feels the discomfort triggered by the perception of a minute behavioural index and responds by withdrawing,[7] avoiding its mother's gaze and putting on the sad face that expresses the dark mood that is coming over it.

A model of the self and models of others take shape at the same time in the inner world of the child. Subsequently, the abused child continues to respond to the representations he has acquired. He resists change and has difficulty in integrating new experiences that might modify his internal models. Except during adolescence, when the inevitable emotional reworking creates a moment when negative representations acquired in childhood can be modified.[8] This is a turning point in the child's life.[9] It is a sensitive period when the emotions are so strong that they enable the biological memory to learn a different emotional style – if the environment gives it the opportunity to do so. A deprived child can subsequently learn to find the emotional security it was denied because the 'establishment of relationships outside the family of origin may alter existing attachment-related postulates'.[10]

Bruno had no idea how dirty he was. He was in care and had been placed as a farmer's boy at the age of seven. The farmer's wife made him sleep on a bale of hay in the barn, together with a 'big' boy of fourteen. Their job was to draw water from the well, light the fire and keep an eye on the sheep. After a few months of paddling around in liquid manure and sleeping in the barn, both boys were covered in a layer of filth that was as black as their clothes. One Sunday, a lady who was acting as a kind of support worker came to treat Bruno to a day inside a real house.[11] But when the nice lady tried to give the little boy a bath, she could not stop herself from showing her disgust. For the first time in his life, Bruno felt that he was filthy. He had a feeling of having a dirty self, and at the same time he was perceived as a model of an other who despised him. It was as though he had thought to himself: 'The gaze of kind adults is teaching me that I am dirty.' From that day onwards, the boy felt at ease only when he was in the company of marginal boys who did not make him feel dirty. He began to avoid kind adults, who soiled him by looking at him. By adapting in this way, Bruno was inserting himself into a world of socialization that blocked his resilience.

The Obligation to Love Differently

In a stable environment where nothing changes and where the stereotype has it that 'a kid in care cannot become anything but a dirty, rough farmer's boy', a child cannot change. It is difficult to acquire a different relational style when nothing changes in either society or the social gaze.

Whether we like it or not, adolescence creates a moment that encourages emotional change. The effect of the hormones triggers a new developmental phase in the nervous system, and this provides a new opportunity for biological learning.[12] The prohibition on incest forces young people to leave their parents to attempt to form new bonds and to avoid anxieties about incest.[13] This new stage in their development means taking a risk which, like any form of change, can lead to either success or failure. Adolescence is a time when young people blossom, but it is also a period in the life cycle when we see a lot of episodes of anxiety.

If we wish to understand how this new sensitive period is regulated, we have to recall that the children who take most pleasure in thinking about and exploring the outside world are those who have acquired a secure attachment. Adolescents revive skills they learned at a very early age so as to quietly leave their families of origin to form the new bond of marriage.

If we consider a population of one hundred adolescents, we find that sixty-six of them display serene bonds in childhood. Even so, fifteen of them will fail to take this corner in life and will become inhibited and anxious. Paradoxically, their environment has concealed their growing anxiety and prevented them from facing up to the problem by providing them with too much security. Too much affection does as much to damage development as emotional deprivation.

Conversely, if we regularly follow up the thirty-four adolescents who experienced an insecure (avoidant, ambivalent or confused) attachment as children, we find to our surprise that ten of them became secure at this point. The young people who underwent this metamorphosis were able, thanks to a girlfriend or close friend, to construct the secure emotional base that their parents were unable to give them.[14]

Half the young people who had a bad start in life

explained their transformation in terms of chance encounters, whilst the others attributed their success to their willingness to meet new people. We can explain the apparent contradiction by saying that raging hormone surges modify the inner world of pubescent young people and make them hypersensitive to information that they previously perceived in a sluggish way. The intense secretion of testosterone in boys suddenly makes them impatient and eager for action, and they react violently to any frustration. In contrast, the gentler but variable secretion of oestrogen in girls sometimes makes them verbally explosive or, the reverse, very tender-hearted.[15]

The whole of this sensitive period invites them to take stock of their capabilities as they prepare for the next ordeal. Young people look back at their past, tell themselves their own stories or explain them to an imaginary court so as to arrive at a better understanding of who they are and of how they can commit themselves. This work gives them access to formal thought and to deductive logic, which, by bringing together scattered data, makes the world coherent. At this point, adolescents become eager to meet people outside their own families. Depending on what their neighbourhood or society has to offer, they will either meet friends who are delinquent or friends who will socialize them. These encounters are not passive, however, as young people actively explore the world around them to find the people and events to which they aspire.

Of the one hundred children who were tracked until adolescence, five of those who got off to a bad start and who were in constant distress went under at this point because they were submerged by the many problems they had to deal with.

This is another way of saying that, if we observe one hundred children, only fifty of the sixty-six who started out with secure attachments will have a happy adolescence. Of the thirty-four children who had a difficult start in life, ten will be just as happy. On the other hand, sixteen of the children who had a good start will end up in the same state as the twenty-four who had a bad start and will have a critical adolescence.[16] Even so, their ability to change is such that, after a few difficult years, thirty of the young people who are in difficulty will stabilize and revert to an easier and more pleasant way of life because they enjoy a sort of natural resilience. Ten, however, will experience severe mental and social problems. In the West, the image of adolescence is wrongly associated with this minority.

Ten tragedies, thirty critical periods and sixty happy adolescents – these young people simply do not correspond to the cultural stereotype that places the emphasis on crises and difficult periods.[17] That cliché tells a partial truth but it leads to a false generalization. It is the case that, with an adolescent population of fourteen million children, this still leaves us with 1.4 million young people in distress.

Given that adolescence normally constitutes a period of emotional reworking in which all young people use what they have learned in the past in order to commit themselves to the future, it is a period that favours the resilience process. Victims of trauma can therefore take advantage of it and embark upon a new and constructive existential adventure.

The emotional style they have acquired and the meaning they have given to their wounds are the mental capital that young people use to represent and respond to their future commitments.[18] As it happens, secure adolescents have many more friends, are older when they first begin to have sexual relations (17.5 years) and have fewer partners (two or three).[19] Adolescents who are afraid of expressing their emotions (avoidant attachment), who are aggressive to those they love because they are anxious (ambivalent attachment), who are happy only when they imprison their love-object (anxious attachment), or who are always in distress (confused attachment) have few friends because they find it difficult to form relationships. They fling themselves into a sexual life over which they have little control in the hope of finding the relationship they are looking for. It is in this population that we find the boys who take careless risks, the girls who fall pregnant at an early age, and the sexually transmitted diseases. These adolescents have lots of partners (seven between the ages of twelve and eighteen). They seek out traumatic events that help to give them a sense of identity and exploit the theatricality of drugs, which at least gives them a role but which almost always inflicts another wound to add to those that were inflicted on them as children. Adolescents with avoidant styles of attachment hide their inner turmoil behind a mask of inhibition; they usually have their first sexual relations relatively late but their sexual awakening will be both unexpected and explosive. It is, on the other hand, in the 'difficult attachment' group that we find the greatest number of emotional changes that set in train a process of resilience.[20]

Child-Mascots and Supermen

There are now 120 million abandoned children wandering the streets all over the world. They have no families and no educational structures. Then there are children suffering from emotional neglect, and the runaways who choose to live on the streets because they find a more eventful life and more affection there than in the comfortable but soulless homes of their nice parents.[21] Most of them are desocialized and have developmental problems, but over 30 per cent of this enormous population will revert to a resilient development, if their deprived emotional structure can be articulated with the emotional structure of either an individual or a group.

Physical abuse is hard to imagine, even though it is readily observable; it is much more difficult to observe emotional neglect. It is difficult to see a non-event, especially when the child who has been hurt has little awareness of what has happened.[22] There is no physical pain and no humiliation. There is no devastating loss. There is just a slow and insidious loss of affection that is all the more damaging in that it is not really a conscious process. When we are dealing with blows, rape, wars or broken attachments we can date the aggression and give it a shape. What we are talking about here is a cooling of the world, a slow extinction and a discreet but continuous erasure of attachment figures.

When a deprived child who has been insidiously damaged in this way becomes old enough to have a close relationship, she grows anxious because a surge of desire is pulling at the edges of a wound that has been badly stitched. She may break down when she falls in love for the first time. For a young person who was able to begin building defences as a child, meeting a lover may, in contrast, signal the beginning of a resilient metamorphosis.

The 'child-mascots' who are found in every

orphanage are a good example. Although they are very distressed, they make us laugh. Although they are very sad, they write poems and give them to us when no one is looking. Although they have been quite abandoned, they weave a network of little friends, and try to support them. These defensive constructs provide emotional bridges in a world that is in ruins. Thanks to their inner defences, these distressed children can preserve a little island of beauty. Taking refuge in daydreams gives them a few hours of the happiness that desperate children seek. It is as though they had a date with some little secret that makes them happy: 'Quick, let's get back to the point I reached in my dream last night.' They plan their future lives by coming up with crazy projects that allow them to put up with the sadness of the real world and with the misery of their day-to-day lives. Their need to understand gives shape to the outside world, and they try not to become cut off from it. They want to see and analyse it in order to control it later 'when I'm grown up'. Their curiosity and mental activity keeps them in touch with it and prevents the melancholic shipwreck they have so narrowly avoided. Their creativity transforms their suffering into the drawings they pass around, the stories they tell, the little plays they act out, and this makes them the centre of attention. The other children in the orphanage gather around them to warm themselves up.

Child-mascots who attract attention are not little supermen. Far from it. But before disaster struck, their environment did leave some early imprints on them and did leave an ember of resilience in their memories.[23] It is as though they were thinking: 'I feel that I can be loved because I know that I was once loved.' The disaster and the spark coexist in their memories, and it is with that self-representation that they commit themselves to the adventure of love.

Aline told me: 'I was ashamed of having no parents. So when a boy approached me, I lied. I invented wonderful parents and talked about them a lot. I lied for a reason. I told him I was horrified by my telephone bill to make him think I had lots of friends. I dreamed of having wonderful parents: a father who was a civil servant, and a mother who stayed at home. But when a boy told me "I love you", I told him to get lost: "You're laughing at me" and I was aggressive towards him.'

Why Leave Those You Love?

Bruno was also responding to a self-image, but his reasoning was that of a boy: 'Even before I felt any sexual desire, I was already attracted to girls. I don't know why, but I kept thinking of something that happened to me when I was ten. I'd stolen something from a bigger boy. He was fourteen. He chased me around the orphanage playground and punched me hard in the face. I felt groggy. A girl ran up to me, put her arms around my neck and said a few kind words to me. I've often replayed that scene in my mind.'

Almost all of the billions of things, actions and words that encircle us will be forgotten and will merge into the environment that surrounds and shapes us without our being aware of it. And then a scenario, whose dramatic action leads to a denouement, suddenly comes to mind and lingers there in the form of a memory. Bruno delighted in recalling this scene because it told him that girls were the bringers of affection. They had the power to make up for losses, and to help him rediscover the trace of a lost love that they could revive. Bruno was therefore a harmless friend until the sudden surge of desire led to a change in his behaviour because it made the company of girls seem so desirable. 'I need affection so badly that, when I approach a girl, I feel I'm taking an enormous risk. It almost scares me. Girls mean so much to me that it seems stupid to say something like: "It's a nice day." Extraordinary things are the only things you can say to a girl, and I can't say them. As soon as I get close to a girl, my self-esteem falls and I feel pathetic. I'm useless. So, the more I love her, the worse I feel. I leave her because that makes me feel better, and it's driving me to despair.'

Boys like this find love difficult because they

have acquired an insecure emotional style. A self-representation such as this leads to commitments that owe nothing to chance: 'The only times I feel happy are when I am in a cemetery or at a funeral. The suffering of others makes me all emotional. When I'm with people who are in pain, I stop feeling abnormal.' The woman who said this to me explained that when she met her future husband, it was love at first sight: 'I fell in love with him at once because he was the saddest.' She then justified her choice of love-object by talking about romanticism, gentleness, and added: 'I've never been frightened of a handsome man. I always want to be aggressive towards men who are cheerful.'

Because of their disrupted life-histories, deprived adolescents tend to over-invest in the emotional domain. They find it so fraught that they begin to be afraid of the opposite sex. 'I feel ill whenever I'm in love,' one deprived boy told me. He then went on: 'I'm frightened of women, and I find myself alone and in despair.' Boys like this dare not go near the girls they desire. Celibacy means different things to boys and girls. For a boy whose adolescence is making a wound inflicted in the past even worse, celibacy means a failed relationship, despair and loneliness. For the adolescent girl who finds herself in a man's bed when all she wanted to do was talk to him, it means emotional instability and aggression born of sexual misunderstandings.

The fact that boys experience celibacy as something painful, whereas girls tend to be oriented towards an aggressive instability, is the result of a series of adaptations. Deprived boys run away from the women they would like to love, whereas deprived girls are aggressive towards the men who take advantage of them.

Flight is a regressive form of adaptation and not a resilience factor because it is a repetition of something and not a development. And yet this emotional vulnerability is still malleable. Many deprived children have been in a lot of institutions over the years, and have developed various relational styles as a result. Depending on the adults they came across, they may have been made a fuss of, rejected, ignored, abused or praised to the skies. Some children always reproduce the same emotional style – affectionate or hostile – but most change their expression to suit the relationship of the moment. Their ability to respond in different ways to those around them proves that we can still learn to love if a new environment provides the emotional stability that gives us time to change.

When society gives damaged young people a few stable cultural structures, such as somewhere to do their homework, clubs where they can meet people, or dreams they can share, we find that many of these attachment-disordered children gradually become more secure and allow themselves to be tamed by the opposite sex. The tendency towards celibacy is less pronounced in groups that are brought together by a political or artistic project. Deprived children find altruism easier than intimacy. But we also find that the emotional vulnerability that made encounters with the opposite sex so painful now becomes a stabilizing factor. It is as though these young people were saying: 'I found it so hard to find a partner that I am willing to pay a high price for going on with this way of loving because I feel that I am slowly getting somewhere.' After a difficult period of settling down, couples like this may do better than those in the population at large.[24] An adolescent who has been hurt finds it easier to be influenced by his partner because he makes progress when he is with her. An adolescent who has not been hurt and whose personality is more stable and settled would resent the love-contract as an attack on his integrity, or as too high a price to pay.

People who are in an emotional mess are unpredictable because the inevitable emotional reworking they feel going on inside them can take them in the opposite direction to the sexual partners they meet. Some partners allow them to pick up the developmental process that was interrupted by the traumatic event; others make things worse. These 'cannibals of love' did acquire an emotional style during their damaged childhood but, at the sensitive moment when their adolescent emotions are being reworked, they will either evolve or go under.

They are as likely to become impulsive delinquents as they are to become virtuous moralists.[25]

The Dawn of Meaning Is Gender-Specific

The lack of symmetry between the sexes is clearer than ever during adolescence because 'pregnancy can be regarded as a normal developmental "crisis" in which the girl becomes her mother's equal, her husband's spouse and her baby's mother'.[26] At this point, the girl feels that her woman's body and her feminine condition are being put to the test: 'Is my body capable of carrying a baby? Will I be the same kind of mother as my mother? Can I rely on my husband?' Over the last generation or so, a few other questions have arisen: 'Will the way society is organized take advantage of this crucial moment and reduce me to my role as mother, or will it allow me to pursue my personal development?' All forms of love are called into question by pregnancy: the style of attachment acquired in childhood, the adolescent reworking of the emotions, and a woman's right either to go on loving herself a little or to stop doing so in order to devote herself to her family.

The same argument can be applied to men, but the physical involvement is not the same. When a mother imagines the baby she is carrying, she feels there are

72

two people inside her, but a boy feels more individualized than ever when he imagines how he will support
his family – or leave it. A lot of spousal abuse begins
during pregnancy because men are afraid: they think
their wives are preparing to build an emotional prison.
'She'll take advantage of her pregnancy to make a
slave of me. She is pretending to devote herself, but
that's just her way of controlling everything.' Anxiety
about being dominated leads to a violent rebellion,
but the contrite husband then begs forgiveness and
therefore gives the power he has just challenged so
brutally back to his wife.[27] This is the beginning of a
process of anti-resilient repetition.

This sensitive period can also take people in quite
the opposite direction. Many helpless young men with
identity problems, who were heading for disaster as a
result of their damaging encounters with other drug-
users, delinquents and drop-outs, can set a more
resilient course when the world takes on a new meaning
because they have become fathers. 'All work bored
me and I thought that only mugs fell into that trap.
I'm happy now and, because I'm working for this
baby's sake, all my efforts mean something. He needs
me. Now I know who I'm getting up for in the
morning.' For this young man, the baby has played
the same role that the cathedral played for the stonebreaker.

These surveys suggest that if a damaged adolescent

is left alone with his wound, there is a strong probability that he will drift into anti-resilient repetition. But the sensitive period created by the emotional reworking of sexual desire[28] or by a pregnancy can be used to help him to become resilient. Twenty-eight per cent of damaged children 'spontaneously' improve during adolescence.[29] What appears to be a natural development in fact corresponds to a constructive encounter with someone who is significant in either emotional, sexual or cultural terms. Certain social groups and institutions have greatly improved on that figure and have an improvement rate of over 60 per cent because they have learned to pay attention to resilience factors.[30]

Even when the dangerous bend of adolescence has been successfully negotiated, it is by no means certain that the resilience effect will last. This is because, given the human condition, no effect can last for ever: you can 'catch' flu, be immunized and fall ill again next year. You can make a fortune and then be ruined. You can make progress with a psychoanalyst and then, a few years later, find yourself back on the couch and dealing with a different problem. Most human determinants are in fact no more than tendencies that orient us towards an existential trajectory or a relational style that makes our journey through life either pleasurable or painful. New sources of life appear at every stage of our existence: the attachment of our earliest years gives way to an upsurge in sexual desire when we reach puberty. We start our families and our social adventure at the same time. When we are older, our acquired wisdom finally allows us to understand why we loved, worked and suffered so much. Every change has to be negotiated. Nothing is predetermined, provided that our prejudices do not prevent us from seeing the constant transactions that go on between the psyche, the real world and society.

There is nothing new about this conflict. For thousands of years it was thought that the social hierarchy was justified by the natural order. It was said that men who were rich and healthy were at the top of the ladder because they were a superior breed.

Children Who Do Not Deserve the Bread and Water They Are Given in Prison

François Dolto was one of the first to state, before the Second World War, that children understand a lot of things long before they can talk. By 1946, Jenny Aubry had been put in charge of the distressed children who had been 'dumped' in the 'Enfants assistés' unit at the Saint-Vincent-de-Paul hospital because their mothers were tubercular, delinquent, divorced or very poor. According to the prevailing constitutionalist theories of the day, individuals were bodies that were either robust or puny. The nurses were told to keep the children clean and well fed but to avoid establishing any emotional relationship with them. In this cultural context, attachment was almost unthinkable. These children were physically healthy but their emotional health had been damaged by the collective assumptions of those around them. 'They grunted and cried but never looked at each other. Some never moved, whilst others rocked backwards and forwards or licked the rails of their cots.'[31] We now know from twenty years of ethological experiments that emotionality is really a peripheral biology, formed by the gestures, crying and words that surround children. Children who are denied this emotional nourishment are destroyed.[32] We then see the appearance of 'the discreet or dramatic symptoms presented by children who have been separated from their families and deprived of their mothers' care'.[33] René Spitz's work on hospitalism, John Bowlby's work on children who had been separated from their mothers, Donald Winnicott's work on maternal deprivation, and Anna Freud and Dorothy Burlingham's work on orphans and infants without families then began to be read in every Faculty of Medicine and Psychology. Jenny Aubry was already saying that 'nothing is predetermined'.[34] She had met Anna Freud and had worked with John Bowlby, the psychoanalyst and ethologist who pioneered research into resilience.[35]

At first, a lot of administrators and politicians had to be convinced that, if no one looked after these deprived children, they would become delinquent or autistic. And then our culture accepted the argument all too easily, and emotional deprivation became the explanation for every disorder. Fifty years on, some believers in destiny still claim that children who have had a bad start in life or who have been stigmatized because of the traumas they have undergone are doomed. Those who believe this join the ranks of the politicians who say that: 'These children don't deserve the bread and water they are given in prison.'[36]

It is difficult to establish a long-term causal relationship but it is clear that, if nothing is done, a group of abandoned children will produce more delinquents than a group of children who have been cared for. But does the delinquency result from maternal deprivation, or from the catastrophic socialization of these abandoned children? Michael Rutter had the idea of following the development of a group of children who had been deprived because their parents, who suffered from mental illness, did not have the strength to look after them. Although the children were deprived of affection, the input of their families' social workers ensured that they were not desocialized and did not become delinquent.[37] Their style of attachment was, however, badly affected by their parents' illness.

Some of them overcame their developmental difficulties but their survival strategies cost them dear.

Carlotta told me: 'The loss of love hurts more than my mother's violence. Because she paid me no attention, I was all alone in the world. I couldn't even learn to dress myself or brush my hair because she never said anything to me.' There was still one star in the dark night of Carlotta's emotional despair: 'I'd have liked to have loved my father more. He was prepared to be loved. But he wasn't there. One day, I got him to give me a cuddle by telling him I had a pain in my tummy. My father was afraid it was appendicitis. I was glad that he was worried. I let them operate on me. I knew it wasn't true. I was eight. Even today, I worry about the way I get people to love me.'

A Constellation with One Star Missing

When the major star in an emotional constellation goes out, as it did in the case of this abusive mother, the child clings to any star that is still shining but learns a particular emotional style.

Abuse provides a readily identifiable point of behavioural reference, at least in our culture. But attachment disorders that result from insidious damage are just as serious. Agathe told me: 'I used to rock until I was dizzy. I couldn't let myself become attached to my nurse. My mother was jealous of her. She was nice at home but she was cold at my nurse's and gave me to understand that loving that nurse was a really naughty thing to do. I stopped rocking the day my brother was placed with the same nurse. He told me: "We'll stay together and get married."' Agathe's world was torn apart because she had to make an impossible choice and was forced to deprive herself of affection so as not to betray her mother. The emotional deprivation, which was described as 'subjective' because both the mother and the nurse loved the child, had its roots in the psyche of a mother who could not bear the fact that her daughter loved someone else. Fortunately, Agathe's brother acted as a resilience tutor in a world where two stars had gone out, and that was enough to fill her inner world. This emotional closeness explains why there are fewer suicides in populations of twins than in the population at large, and why couples find it easier to overcome life's ordeals than people who are single.

It is the emotional presence that matters. Its effects are felt even when nothing is said. That is why so many deprived children invest so much in their pets. 'It's my dog who comforts me. I think of him when I'm sad. I talk to him for hours.' Joëlle had in fact been married for five years, but the familiar presence of her dog had become imprinted on her memory.

The young woman used to say: 'Whenever I feel miserable, I turn to my dog for consolation. It's easier to love a dog than a husband.' Affection was in fact so important to her that the slightest upset resulted in separation anxiety, but her dog always responded when she turned to it for affection.

"'My boy!" said the old gentleman, leaning over the desk. Oliver started at the sound. He might be excused for doing so: for the words were kindly said; and strange sounds frighten one. He trembled violently, and burst into tears."[38] Charles Dickens is explaining to us that unexpected kindness can be frightening! This is a long way from the linear arguments that automatically assume that, because emotional deprivation causes serious disorders, love is all that is needed to take away the pain. *Oliver Twist* suggests something very different. My experience of life suggests to me that a wretched child with no emotional relationships who worked ten hours a day in a blacking factory in nineteenth-century England must have experienced utter despair when he was given an unexpected sign of the affection he needed so badly. Carlotta confirms that this is the case: 'As soon as someone loves me, I attach so much importance to it and want so much to satisfy them that I worry about disappointing them. So I reject people who love me. If I'm rejected, the anxiety goes away and I will find it easier to die.' In her everyday language, she was telling me that love made her anxious and that, when she felt unloved, the anxiety went away and she just drifted – towards death.

When a man did love her, Carlotta became aggressive towards him. And then she was reduced to despair because she had made him unhappy. She could not understand why, when she had been so nice to the mother who had mistreated her, she reduced a man who wanted so much to love her to such a pitiful state. She did not love her mother and adored this man but, because she had not learned to control her affections, she could not give him the kind of love that was acceptable within a relationship. Her kindness towards her mother was nothing more than a strategy she used to disarm the enemy, and her brutality towards the man she loved was nothing more than a reaction to the anxiety caused by love.

Many surprising forms of behaviour in fact result from the insidious childhood acquisition of styles of attachment. Jean-Marie writes: 'I looked at her body, and she was gorgeous as it happens . . . she whispered in my ear: "I'll bet you can make me come . . ." "Come", the word terrified me because I didn't know how nice it can be . . . I left without even thinking about how disappointed she'd be. If I ever see her again, I'll tell her I'm sorry.'[39] The expression 'time to learn to live' briefly summarizes the hope that resilience can bring. We can always learn to live, or learn

81

again if we have died. It is not until later that 'it will be too late'.[40]

Spoilt Children, Rotten Fruit

A spoilt child can learn to love differently, and this explodes into illogical behaviour in adolescence. This emotional deformation may be attributable to either a lack of affection or a surfeit of affection. It is in fact only when we are observing the parent–child relationship from the outside that we can speak of 'too much affection'. It is as though we were watching a film. We see parents devoting themselves to their children, thinking of no one else, showering them with gifts and organizing their entire adult lives around their children's games and entertainment. But when we try to imagine what the children are feeling, we come to understand that, in their inner world, being loved in this way means being prevented from loving anyone else. They are emotional prisoners. 'Too much affection' does not mean that there is a surfeit of affection. On the contrary, it is a prison that leads to a sort of deprivation. This numbness is not very different from the emotional deprivation experienced by children who have been abandoned. A surfeit of affection is impoverishing because the over-abundance of stimuli leads to a sensory monotony that sends the soul to sleep and prevents us from desiring anything. A lack of affection leads to despair and makes us feel that there is no point in going on living, but living in an emotional prison dulls and destroys the pleasure of exploring. 'Whenever my mother was nice to me, I told her to get lost because her way of loving was suffocating me.' This emotional mode asphyxiates us and prevents us from learning the lessons of everyday life: 'When I got too much attention, I felt oppressed. My mother was still cutting up my meat for me when I was fourteen, and my grandmother was still doing it when I was nineteen. When I was an adolescent, I had to discourage them to make myself feel better . . . I made myself fail. And now they're sick of me and they leave me alone: "It's your life." I find that liberating. It takes a weight off my mind.'

When children who have been traumatized dream of becoming perfect parents who can give their children all the things they never had, they do not realize that nothing is more imperfect than a perfect parent. The mistakes and errors that so enrage children teach them to be confrontational. A parental mistake is an invitation to autonomy. 'It's up to me to look after myself now because my mother's going the wrong way about it. My parents' affection for me knew no bounds. They adored me. I'd rather they'd just loved me. I'd like to have been badly brought up, to have had a few smacks. That would have allowed me to rebel. Instead, my day-to-day life was bland because my parents did everything for me.'

A child who survives living in an environment where there is no affection is his own external object, and his only external object. As there is no otherness, there is no outside and no inside and the child becomes very self-centred. Loving someone else means worrying about the unknown. Conversely, a child whose environment smothers him with affection also learns to become the centre of the universe because she does not need to discover the internal space of others. There is no otherness here either, and therefore no subject. For a child like this, affection means 'the prison of what I know' and 'lack of interest in the unknown'. This type of emotional structure kills desire.

Although they look very different, both these emotional impasses are the result of impoverishment, and we have to ask ourselves how children who have been loved in this way will learn to love. Children placed in emotional isolation always end up by accentuating their self-centred behaviour (rocking, self-harming, masturbation). They adapt to their deprivation and suffer less because they become indifferent to it. A non-verbal presence can be enough to modify the way they express their emotions, provided that it is stable enough to become familiar. It allows them to take a new interest in life and to open themselves up to others, sometimes with excessively intense anger or an anxious attachment.[41] Because they have invested so much in any bonds they may have with their surrogate parents, and then with their friends, partners and children, they are subsequently able to work on their own resilience. Their emotional feverishness imbues their partners with a particular sensation that can often be exasperating but which can also afford them the pleasure of acting as a resilience-tutor.

Prisoners of emotion who have grown up in an emotional hothouse also become self-centred because they do not need to invest in others. For them, there is no visible trauma. Nothing has been broken because they never constructed anything. This is equivalent to a traumatic collapse, but without the collapse. When deprived children say: 'No one ever gave me anything but I've managed to make something of myself all the same,' they feel that they have won a minor victory or have begun to be resilient. But if they have been smothered with love, they think: 'They didn't equip me for life . . . they gave me everything and I've done nothing with it.' Their self-esteem is poor and the only relief they can find is by being aggressive to those who are close to them. They find it difficult to be resilient because it is only later, or during adolescence, that they can identify their devoted aggressor. Because they do not know who to confront, they are not good at standing up for themselves. Violent rebellion is their only road to personalization.

The Strange Freedom of Giant Babies

Emotional deprivation teaches us a way of loving that can change if we meet the right people, whereas emotional prisons imbue us with what appears to be a more permanent relational tendency. Vulnerable parents who are too attached to their children create little old men and women who adapt to their developmental tutors by becoming their parents' parents.[42] But parents who smother their children with too much affection are displaying the symptoms of a parental vulnerability that tutors a different style of development and produces 'giant babies'.[43] It seems that the modern technological and psychological world encourages such developments by relativizing identification with parental models and organizing families and societies whose attachments are both multiple and broken. The technology that allows parents to work far away from home and organizes short and varied attachments destroys one-to-one relationships and prevents adults from imprinting themselves on their children's memories. These 'big babies', who are well cared for in social and material terms, remain charming, greedy, passive and fearful, and oscillate between the joys of the baby's bottle and the anger of frustration. This system is very different from the multi-attachment system in which bonds last long enough to become imprinted upon children's memories. In an emotional prison, there is only one permanent bond, and that numbs the child and cuts it off from the world. In an emotional desert, a little warmth is imprinted on the child from time to time. The two systems are similar: the child can do no more than glean a few scraps of affection from here and there.

As with any form of deprivation, when the sudden appearance of sexual desire makes these adolescents want to find someone to love, they fear that they will become dependent on those who are ready to love them.

John Bowlby was one of the first to try to understand these paradoxical problems: children who are the 'centre of the world' grow up to be emotionally deprived and form relationships by submitting to others. The British psychoanalyst cites a study of a small group of twenty-six six-year-old children who were so anxious that they could not be separated from their mothers.[44] Some adults interpreted their behaviour as a proof of love: 'My God, these children love their mums so much.' Others found it disturbing: 'Still tied to their mother's apron strings.' Six of these emotionally dependent children came from stable homes where their mothers did everything for them. Fourteen had a very unsettled home life and were passed back and forth like parcels between their mothers, grandmothers, neighbours and professional carers. Eleven of the fourteen had acquired an anxious attachment because there was no time to establish a bond. Seventeen of the twenty-six children had acquired a dependent style of loving, either because they became isolated as a result of being smothered with affection (six of the twenty-six), or because they were prevented from loving because they were, with the encouragement of our modern social system, entrusted to surrogate attachment-figures (eleven of the twenty-six). When they tracked these children, who had been unable to learn the secure attachment that allows us to love without becoming depersonalized, until they reached adolescence, the researchers found that they established the same type of bond with their friends and their first loves: 'He's wonderful. He can do everything better than I can. All I can do is follow him.' The only way these fearful adolescents could escape their anxiety about incest was by surrendering to a friend or lover. They thought they could gain their independence if they followed someone in order to get away from their families of origin.

These adolescents' self-esteem was poor: 'I feel secure only when I'm with someone I love, and I imitate their behaviour and ideological values because it's a way of staying close to them.' All the adolescents who 'chose' this strange autonomy had suffered separation anxiety as children.[45] It is as though they were saying to themselves: 'If I submit, I can stay close to the one I love. I feel safe and I can leave my parents without feeling the anxiety of finding myself alone in an emotional desert.' The paradoxical thing about these 'giant infants' is that they acquire their freedom through submission. Perhaps this explains the strange choices made by well-brought-up youngsters who have been well treated by their generous parents who suddenly decide to join a fundamentalist religion or an extremist party. They say, 'Wearing the veil is my choice,' rather as though they were saying, 'I'll find my freedom by getting myself put in prison.' A minority of these adolescents have experienced real separation, repeated losses or never-ending periods of mourning. But most of them had a childhood in which they identified so closely with their mothers that they were prevented from developing any personality of their own. So they discovered the ersatz solution of the veil or the extremist slogan because it represented a social commitment that allowed them to tear themselves away from their families, whilst still remaining part of a closely knit social group. The only way these adolescents, who felt secure only when they clung to their parents, could resist their incestuous feelings was by making extreme choices: because they had submitted, there was always someone who was there for them.

Emotionally deprived children are submissive because submission allows them to remain in contact with people who are willing to love them. A child who has experienced a surfeit of affection will submit to an attachment-figure from outside the family of origin in order to ward off their anxiety about incest whilst also avoiding the fear of the unknown.

In his theory of spoilt children, Freud writes that 'neuropathic parents, who are inclined as a rule to display excessive affection, are precisely those who are most likely by their caresses to arouse the child's disposition to neurotic illness'.[46] We are therefore not talking about excessive parental affection, but about a non-conscious process that teaches the child to be anxious about loss. Something is transmitted by the insidious reality of everyday actions. No matter whether it is a real loss due to death, illness, separation or a compensatory over-investment, the damage done to the child's style of loving always leads to an impoverishment of its perceived reality. The 'how' of the parents' behaviour, or their way of touching, smiling, attracting or rejecting, does more to shape the development of the child than the 'why', which leads to either isolation or emotional fusion. Very different 'whys' can provoke the same 'how'. 'I am ashamed of the way I hate my child, so I'm going to take great care of him' constructs the same perceived world as 'I only feel good about myself when I'm looking after my child' or 'I'm going to give her everything because I had nothing'. In all these cases, the sensorial reality that tutors the child's development has been damaged.

If we wish to restart a resilience process in children who have been torn apart by an insidious trauma, we have to work on both them and their families. The mother must be made to feel so secure that she can use something other than her child for self-reassurance. We often have to involve the husband by helping the mother to discover that he too is an individual and by asking him to become involved in day-to-day tasks so as to enrich the sensory environment and to open the gates of the emotional prison. If we can do this, 'there is a good prospect not only of helping those who have grown up insecure but of preventing others from becoming so'.[47]

Children Lay Down the Law

When technology modifies cultures, as it is beginning to do all over the world, cultural pressures no longer structure families in the same way. The death of the paterfamilias inverts the life-debt. Children no longer owe their parents their lives; on the contrary, it is the children who give the parental couple a meaning. It is no longer the father who pronounces prohibitions; it is the child. Simply by coming into the world, children prohibit their parents from separating or, rather, order them to make an effort to stay together. Two generations ago, women wanted to give their husbands children. Now they want to give their children a father. Family values are being constructed around children. The 'passion for childhood' which organizes the emotional environment of American children, and which is now spreading to Europe, produces infants with a hypertrophied narcissism: 'It's him who gives the orders now.'[48] 'Trapped by the impossibility of separation, and forced to be satisfied with, or even trapped into an impossible debt if he attempts to become autonomous in respect to and in opposition to parents who are beyond reproach, the child can demonstrate his difference only through a violent rejection.'[49] This violence sometimes leads to terrifying situations, but it tells us something about a culture which, because it wants to do away with all the ordeals of normal development, denies children any feeling of victory and inflicts an emotional disaster on their families. I refer to battered parents.

'When, ten years ago, we discovered to our stupefaction, that adults could be at the mercy of children who battered and threatened them, our findings were greeted with scepticism on the part of our colleagues and incredulity on the part of the public.'[50] This scepticism is a standard reaction on the part of those who see only what the official narratives tell them. Our educational system encourages us to use our intelligence in this way because it promotes those who can trot out what it teaches them. What exists in the real world, but not in representations of the real world, cannot be seen by excellent students who see only what they already know. Those who came back from the death camps found it difficult to talk about what had happened there.[51] Michel Manciaux has described how members of the Académie de médecine expressed doubts about the reality of child abuse. Marceline Gabel and Judge Rosenveig have described their disputes with the great names of psychoanalysis, who insisted that incest did not exist in the real world and was simply the fantasy fulfilment of a wish.

In the space of a single generation, parental abuse has become a worldwide phenomenon. In the United States, 25 per cent of all calls to abuse helplines are made by battered parents. The very high figures recorded in France and Québec reveal that this is both a real phenomenon and one that is difficult to talk about, as the victims feel a need to call for help but often refuse to go to the police or to press charges against their own children. The Japanese were the first to identify the problem: 'girls and boys become uncontrollable when they reach adolescence.'[52] Cuddly children who were conformist and good at school and who seemed to have a serene attachment-style suddenly become violent after a minor family incident: 'Look away when you give me anything to eat . . . Get down on your hands and knees when I come home from school.' This extreme behaviour alternates with 'sudden bouts of infantile regression, tears . . . demands to be fed with liquids'. The explanation for the rising number of big babies in Japan is that an immense socio-cultural upheaval has transformed family structures and over-invested in children, who are adored at home and terrified of at school. Technology has given women more leisure time and greater power – and husbands are working longer hours to make more money so as to ensure that their families have more luxuries and live in greater comfort.[53] The technological revolution and changing habits supplied the 'big baby' with a model that made him forget that his father was working on his behalf and led him to believe that his mother spent her time keeping him entertained.

The same phenomenon has occurred in China, where the 'one child' law has so changed children's development that little angels have turned into a generation of very unhappy domestic tyrants. Within the space of a single generation, there has been an incredible increase in the number of hyperactive boys who leave their parents exhausted. Children are becoming obese and suicidal, and they are reduced to despair because their lives are problem-free.[54]

When Love Is Above the Law

Children with siblings usually find ways of imposing strict limits on how far they can express their desires. But an only child or a child who has been smothered with affection cannot learn how to be inhibited.[55] When its father is absent, dead or works too much, and when its mother decides to devote her life to her big baby, the daily rituals that teach children the art of not doing whatever they like no longer exist. An act becomes a source of immediate satisfaction rather than a preparation for a project. Eating, sleeping, playing and hitting now fill the mental world of adolescents and their environment prevents them from learning to be inhibited.

This phenomenon has often been observed in generations born after great technological and cultural revolutions. The figures are not, as yet, very accurate as they depend to some extent on the definitions used, but it is estimated that between 5 and 16 per cent of children in the United States are abusive;[56] the figures for Japan and France are 4 per cent and 0.6 per cent respectively.[57]

When a group of us got together to collate this scattered data, we were able to establish a cohort of over one hundred parents who had been assaulted by their adolescent children.[58] We decided to exclude parents who had been assaulted by psychotic children who had no image of what a father should be, elderly parents who had been abused by their grown-up children, and matricides and patricides, because the act of violence could not be repeated.

There were almost as many abusive girls (40 per cent) as there were boys (60 per cent). The Grenoble team did not come up with the same findings, and found three times more boys than girls.[59] Sixty per cent of all abusive adolescents had their *baccalauréat*, 50 per cent had been to university and 5 per cent had become university lecturers. After a few hellish years, most of our abusive adolescents had left their families to live in boarding schools, rented accommodation or with friendly families.

There were few adopted children in the cohort. The emotional development of the few adopted abusers was comparable with that of abusers living with their birth families. Almost all were conformist and anxious children until they became adolescents who made cruel unconscious demands: 'unliveable with at home and adorable outside the home . . . until there was violence within the family; when their parents punish them, they complain that they are being abused . . .'[60] It is therefore not adoption that makes the difference, but the development of children who conformed because they were anxious, and who then became unconsciously tyrannical adolescents.

The abused parents were very old. Almost all of them enjoyed a high social status, and an astonishing number (30 per cent) were lawyers, doctors and psychologists (20 per cent). Almost all of them were highly educated and had stated their intention of giving their children a democratic upbringing.[61] We found that 20 per cent were single mothers; that figure is high, but the Chartiers found 60 per cent. The statistical variations occur because the data was gathered in different places. Parental couples find it easier to consult therapists on a private basis, whereas single mothers, in a state of personal and social despair, are more likely to be encountered in centres for difficult adolescents.

Bitter Freedom: A Comedy in Three Acts

When a woman brings a child into the world, what Winnicott describes as 'the first hundred days of being madly in love' constitutes a moment of enthralment in which mother and child 'learn each other' very quickly because they are so sensitized to each other. Once that moment has passed, the family system prevents the child from being put in an emotional prison because a third party – the father or grandmother – is present. At later stages, the nursery, school and neighbourhood will intervene. When the child reaches adolescence, university or work will play the same role. A so-called 'single' mother may not be isolated; she may have a man, a mother, friends or other institutions in her life. Such a single mother does not go into prison with her child, and such one-parent families are not toxic.

Conversely, a parental couple can create a closed home in which there are no rituals, to which no friends are ever invited and which is not involved in any social adventure. This often happens in households where incest occurs. Even when no transgressive acts occur, such physical and emotional proximity creates a whiff of incest or an incestuous atmosphere that young people try to escape through hatred or physical violence.

None of the abusive adolescents I have met had the opportunity to experiment with this separation effect. When they were old enough to experience their first sexual desires, they were living in a curiously structured world in which they had to make an impossible choice between a family environment that was so protective as to be nauseating, and a social adventure that frightened them into an anxious paralysis. Whereas the cultural stereotype insists that an abused child will grow up to be an abusive parent, many (58 per cent) of the over-permissive parents who loved their children to pieces had themselves been abused as children.

Without meaning to, those parental couples who over-invested in their children because of their own painful histories had built an emotional prison.

The sudden upsurge of sexual desire forces young people to leave their parents on pain of experiencing terrifying anxieties. When, however, her culture provides a mother with a man, a family, a neighbour-hood and a society that can invite her children to move away by suggesting to them that they should continue their development and embark on an adventure outside their family of origin, there is no possibility of building an emotional prison. When they are separated and individualized in this way, adolescent boys can go on loving their mothers in peace because there is no sexual element in their attachment and because they are learning to love other women in different ways. The same is true of adolescent girls who, thanks to this process of distancing and separation-individual-ization, no longer think that their fathers desire them or that their mothers are preventing them from loving anyone else.

When the parents' history or the social context leads them to create a closed emotional field, the separation effect is based upon hatred. In some cases, the mother is heroic and the father is sacrificed. The mechanisms of emotional enthralment make it quite impossible for the children to get away and create an exasperating cocoon surrounded by a menacing social context. In situations like this, adolescents take refuge in the family that is stifling them because their social environment is either threatening or empty. Because they are smothered by their gilded deprivation, they can neither experience lack nor fill the void with dreams, aspirations and desires. This kind of reality kills hope. The adolescent loses in life and cannot be bothered to fight. When a young person who is mired in his past and who has no dreams for the future becomes old enough to have sex, he becomes disillusioned with his parents. 'You did not equip me for life, and you turned me into a dependant.' That is how he will criticize the parents who gave him so much. The giant babies who were brought into the world by our technological culture and our worship of childhood grow up to be domestic tyrants, but they are socially submissive. Their parents' morbid kindness was a control mechanism, and this way of loving leads to emotional misunderstandings: 'My parents make me anxious because they give me everything. They know how to live, but I only know how to take.'

Honorine explained to me how, after the idyll of her earliest years, her mother's wish to be beyond reproach led her to hate her: 'She would get a glass of milk ready for me in the morning and put my pyjamas in the oven to warm them up before putting me to bed. I expected her to do everything for me. I worshipped her. And then, when I was twelve, I suddenly began to hate her. If I was bad at spelling, it was my mother's fault because I expected her to do everything for me: all she had to do was give me lessons, but she didn't do that. It was her fault that I couldn't spell.' José also experienced the same reversal of love to hatred. 'My mother meant the world to me. I was always by her side. When I was twelve, I felt that she was intruding. "You're beginning to grow hairs." When she interfered with my sexuality, I found her repulsive. I had to push her away. She still loved me, but from that day on she stifled me and filled me with anxiety. It was a loving hell. I wish she'd died. Then I wouldn't have needed to hate her.'

Twenty years later, Honorine and José discovered that the invasive behaviour of their parents was the result of their past histories. 'I didn't even know that my mother had been abused,' Honorine told me, whilst José explained: 'I didn't know them. I didn't know who they were. I had no idea of what they thought about life. When I was twenty-five, I learned by chance that my mother had lost her family in the Spanish Civil War, that she had been put in prison as a child and had had to run away and work as a washerwoman to put herself through college. She wanted so much for me to be happy that she never told me anything about all that. I'd have loved her differently if she'd told me. Because she wanted so much to protect me, she ruined [*gâché*] everything for me . . . hid [*caché*] everything from me,' he added, suddenly puzzled by his slip of the tongue.

As in the classical theatre, the comedy of the emotional prison is a play in three acts. After the idyll of Act I, which creates a mushy identity, the loving hell of Act II depicts a violent and desperate bid for autonomy. Act III is about a bitter freedom. A mother says: 'My daughter hit me one day. The next day, I went out and bought myself some jewellery. And to think I'd spent fifteen years saving every penny so that she could have everything.' A mother sighs: 'The day my daughter slapped me, I felt something die inside me . . . I'd just turned down an offer of promotion that would have made me commercial director in another town, so that she wouldn't have to change her dance school. I felt that I'd been set free, and I felt terribly sad.'

Prisons of the Heart

The social prognosis for abusive adolescents is strange. They often find jobs in which violence is structured by the law. They become lawyers, police officers or debt-collectors. These domestic tyrants, who were once conformist children, calm down when they become adults. They become part of a system and accept all its values. This is another form of submission, as they accept everything without ever making the slightest criticism of the discourses, emblems and rules that allow them to take their place in a hierarchical system. Even when they claim to be revolutionaries or terrorists, they submit to a cultural narrative and learn it by heart – word for word – and avoid all thoughts that might give them the freedom to have doubts. Having been emotional captives as children, they now willingly submit to a narrative. They are relieved when they submit to it because a prison – emotional or verbal – gives them the security that comes from being certain.

Having let themselves be talked into things by their devoted parents, they now become the prisoners of a social representation that claims to resolve all their problems. Their violent behaviour within the family was a bid for autonomy and it allowed them to fight their anxieties about incest. But once that danger is gone, these young people, who once submitted to their parents' emotional ascendancy, submit to the culture that surrounds them. This pattern is a good illustration of anti-resilience because young people who have been shaped in this way can neither regain their freedom nor pursue some other form of development. The inexorable process whereby the subject repeats what he or she has learned, demonstrates that a traumatic shock, which is easy to see and easy to understand, can do more to introduce factors that encourage resilience than an insidious trauma that is inscribed in the memory. The latter initiates a non-conscious learning process which, because it inhibits development, blocks resilience.

'Of the fifty young people who, as adolescents, went through a rebellious phase and challenged everything, roughly twenty narrowly avoided involvement in socially unacceptable forms of acting out. And then they matured, found jobs and got married . . . They forget that they were so aggressive and rebellious . . . say that everything was fine . . . and criticize the young people around them because they are uneducated!'[62]

Those young people have transformed their relationships thanks to a resilience process, whereas those Michel Lemay describes as 'gilded but deprived' repeatedly surrender and become powerful thanks to a non-resilience process. The family and social trajectory of Adolf Hitler illustrate the trajectory taken by these submissive tyrants.

The characteristic feature of the first stages in the construction of Adolf Hitler's personality is the chaos surrounding his origins. His grandfather Nepomuk was also the grandfather of his mother Klara.[63] His father Alois, a well-respected customs officer, had a particularly chaotic private life and married three times. One of his wives was richer and older than him, but the other two were of the same generation as his daughters. Before Alois could marry Klara, they had to be granted a dispensation by Rome, as they were first cousins. 'For long after their marriage, Klara could not get out of the habit of calling him Uncle.'[64] These tangled kinship structures and this 'incestuous' genealogy[65] probably created a muddled and poorly individualized representation in the young Adolf's mind.

The household in which he spent his earliest years was overshadowed by painful memories of children who had died. Adolf, who was Klara's fourth child, was the first to survive. A younger brother also died. Alois knocked Klara and his children about, but spent little time at home because he took little interest in his family. Klara's only source of happiness was Adolf: 'she bestowed a smothering, protective love on her two surviving children, Adolf and Paula'.[66] Both she and her younger sister Paula were over-protective of Adolf. Eduard Bloch, the family's Jewish doctor, stated that 'his love for his mother was his outstanding feature . . . I have never witnessed a closer attachment'.[67] Hitler would subsequently state in *Mein Kampf* that 'I had honoured my father, but loved my mother.'[68] When he died in his bunker, he still had a photograph of her on him.

During the 'painful transitional period' of adolescence, Adolf found it so difficult to become autonomous that, to his teachers' astonishment, he would trek every day from his home in Leonding to his school in Linz so as not to be separated from his mother for too long: 'The happy, playful youngster of the primary school days had grown into an idle, resentful, rebellious, sullen, stubborn and purposeless teenager',[69] 'and his behaviour betrayed clear signs of immaturity',[70] writes the historian Ian Kershaw, who was granted permission to work in the Berlin archives. He is describing a 'giant baby'.

Imagine what would have happened if Adolf, a passive adolescent who suddenly exploded, had lived in Africa, where a fourteen-year-old boy had to demonstrate his physical courage before he could join the group, or amongst the Inuit, where he would have had to hunt and fish on the ice and then invent games in order to become socialized. Suppose he had come to France, like the children of the Italian and Polish immigrants of the 1930s. Boys of twelve had to go down the mine in the full knowledge that they would rarely see daylight again. These communities demanded extreme physical abnegation and great interpersonal skills of their young people. The adolescent Adolf would have been of no value because he would have had no social significance. But in a historical context where pan-Germanism used scorn and sarcasm as organizational principles, this big boy, who was both lazy and insolent, received such a good welcome that he became a spokesman for a culture of arrogance. The young Adolf Hitler flourished in a specific sociohistorical context and challenged both the ego-ideal that every culture offers its young people and the values it fosters, which favour individuals who conform to its discourse.

Repetition or Liberation?

These reflections on anti-resilience illustrate the phenomenon of repetition observed by psychoanalysts. The resilience process, in contrast, consists in not submitting to the family, institutional or cultural discourses that predict failure: 'Given what happened to him he's screwed up for life . . . He has no family, so how do you expect him to concentrate on his homework? . . . She's been raped, so she'll never be anything but frigid or a prostitute . . .'

As early as the 1940s, psychoanalysts were beginning to make a distinction between the phenomenon of neurotic repetition, which makes us slaves of our past, and the working-off mechanisms that allow us to escape it. The compulsion to repeat is frequently observed in clinical practice; some people constantly reproduce the situation that causes them to suffer, rather as though some force was making them act illogically: 'She's gone back to that gang, and she'll be sexually assaulted again . . . He suffered because he was abused and perhaps he is now suffering because he is an abusive father . . .' Freud, who was the first to discover this phenomenon, spoke of an uncontrollable process originating in the unconscious. The pleasure principle could not explain it because this quest for unhappiness was motivated by the death drive: 'the absurd violence of repetition in traumatic neuroses'.[71] And it is the case that, after a shattering event, some people can no longer resolve the problems that arise in their everyday lives because they no longer know what they are capable of doing or how they should organize their lives. Because they are drowning, they can no longer face up to the situations they have to live with.

One of the characteristic features of a psychotrauma is the way that images of horror constantly invade the conscious mind by day and reappear in dreams at night. Time stands still because anyone who has been traumatized constantly experiences the horror 'as though it had just happened'. Despite herself, a woman repeats what she has suffered. A man who has suffered violence becomes violent, and the man who has been humiliated seeks to humiliate others. In most cases, the psychotrauma fades away when the traumatized individual goes back to his family or social group. In a variable number of cases, however, it persists and poisons the individual's life. Its effects can take different forms, ranging from 'banal' depression and a loss of interest in life to a physical feeling of painful sadness, disturbed sleep, vulnerability to infection, incipient drug addiction, or the reliving of the traumatic event, which constantly forces itself into the conscious mind. The statistics are also variable, and depend upon where and when the survey was carried out and on how the data was collected. Some trauma victims find it easier to talk about their pain over the phone rather than in face-to-face conversations, precisely because they do not want to lose face.[72] On the whole, we usually find that, six months after the actual trauma, 10 per cent (6 per cent of men and 13 per cent of women) of the casualties are still suffering from psychotraumas. This pathology is the fourth most common form of mental illness.

How practitioners explain this phenomenon depends on how they were trained. Psychoanalysts are not comfortable with the notion of a death drive.[73] Freud claimed that the death drive extended beyond the pleasure principle, and that the repressed drive returned in dreams, symptoms and actions. It is not impossible that this explanation in fact corresponds to a theoretical verbalization of a very difficult period in Freud's own professional life. He had never experienced so many therapeutic failures and was beginning to have doubts about his own practice.[74] The way his patients relapsed completely undid the therapeutic effect of his psychoanalytic interpretations. For many of his patients, analysis had become a neurotic gain. The most important point, however, is that this concept, which Freud elaborated in 1920, or just after the First World War, describes a psychotrauma as a real event and not as a fantasy. In these terrible conditions, Freud was trying to understand his own trauma: a nephew killed in the war, the death of Anton von Freund, a patient with whom he had developed a friendship, the suicide of his pupil Viktor Tausk, the terrible death of his daughter Sophie and her son, whom he loved dearly. Is it possible that Freud was theorizing his own depression?[75] As he could not escape his suffering, he saw repetition everywhere. His suffering was of course real and resulted from the war, the death of his children and of the psychoanalysts who committed suicide, his therapeutic failures, and the fact that his consulting room was empty. Freud was probably protecting himself from his own despair by theorizing wildly and generalizing on the basis of a true account of a period that had been cruel to him.

This is not to say that there is no such thing as repetition. There may, however, be other ways of understanding it and, from the resilience point of view, there may also be ways of avoiding it. 'My mother couldn't catch me because I was too fast for her. So she would wait till I had gone to sleep, come into my room at night, and hit me with a belt . . . I didn't get any affection, so I can't give any. In fact, I dare not tell my daughter that I love her. So I sacrifice myself for her sake. I use the way I behave to say what I can't put into words. I give her things on the sly, without saying a word. I hope she'll understand.' Repeating the clumsy transmission of affection is a defensive strategy which blocks self-expression and distorts emotional relations between mother and daughter. This leads to emotional misunderstandings. In this example, her compulsion to repeat forces the mother to display an avoidant attachment which is distant and perhaps cold because she is afraid to verbalize her affection for her daughter. The daughter is living with an adult who has adopted the stance of a dominated adult who is devoting herself to her child by giving in to her. The girl will have to grow up before she can understand the meaning of this behavioural strategy. And given that her mother's withdrawal has turned her child into a big baby, it will probably be several decades before she understands what this means.

Governed by Our Self-Image

The problem might be regarded as a process of imprinting or an unconscious learning process that facilitates a relational tendency. His everyday interaction with others teaches the child to respond to his idea of 'what he is like with others'. All living creatures inevitably react to perceptions, but from the age of six months onwards a human infant also responds to the representation of 'what I am with others' that was constructed when it was imprinted on his memory.[76] A new-born infant cannot survive unless there are attachment-figures around it. If it is left to its own devices, there is no chance that it will develop. Given the spontaneous nature of biological phenomena, the attachment-figure is almost always the mother who gave birth to it. But anyone who is willing to look after a new-born infant – another woman, a man or an institution – can take on the function of an attachment-figure made up of the images, sense-perceptions and actions that have been addressed to the infant. The repetition of gestures imprints a sensed reality on the child's memory and teaches it to expect certain behaviours from its attachment-figures. A mother who is unhappy because of her personal history, her husband or her social context will display the sensoriality of a depressed woman: her face will be inexpressive and she will not play physical games. She does not look at anyone directly and her voice is lifeless. Living in a sensorial environment that reflects the mental world of its mother, the baby learns to react by withdrawing.[77] As it reaches the end of its first year of life, it has only to perceive this unhappy attachment-figure to expect her to interact as a sad mother. A baby does not just react to what it perceives: it reacts to what it is looking for and anticipates what it has learned.

A child of three, who is now old enough to empathize, is able to respond to its own representation of the representations of its mother's mental world, her motives, her intentions and even her beliefs: 'She'll think it was me that ate the chocolate again, but it was my brother.' A baby who grows up in this glacial world expects others to be cold towards it. It is as though it were thinking: 'All emotional relationships lead to coldness.' Conversely, a child who feels loved believes it is lovable because it has been loved. Because that perception was imprinted on its memory by the banal gestures involved in survival, it gives the child a trusting and lovable self-image, and it responds to that image when it embarks on a relationship.

This learning process gives rise to a long-term emotional style that finds expression in our first close relationships:[78] 'When I think of what I am, I expect she'll turn me down.' Another young man might be thinking: 'When I think of what I am, I think she will accept me.' This image of 'me with someone else' is a construct that depends on who we meet, but, like all phenomena relating to memory, it can change and can be erased, reinforced or transformed.

Shaped by Our Memories, We Shape Our Memories

This type of learning process is a memory without representations. It leads to the acquisition of a bodily or mental aptitude that is not necessarily conscious. We are talking about a procedural memory: sense data shapes the neurological zone of the cortex that handles visual, sonic or kinetic types of data. The brain therefore becomes preferentially sensitized to that type of data. Because this data was perceived at a very early stage, it is more easily perceived than other types of data.

The same argument can be applied to the historical events that make up our narrative identity. But at this level of the construction of the personality, our memory is no longer biological. It is episodic and semantic, and therefore conscious by definition. This 'autobiography' consists of memories of images and anecdotes that can be located in both time and relationships. This type of memory means that we have a self-image that we can evoke intentionally: 'I remember how, when I was six, they were looking everywhere for me. I'd hidden so that I could eat a tomato I'd stolen. I was covered in tomato.' Our semantic memory consists of more general statements:

'I've always been bad at maths.' Our life-projects and our involvement in day-to-day interpersonal relations correspond to these self-images. The subject reacts to this memory construct and not to the return of the actual past. The notion of a script that can be broken down into sequences of images and dialogue is implicit in the unfolding of a history which transforms our emotional, behavioural and verbal responses, and which gives our self-image a narrative form.[79]

On the one hand, our declarative or explicit memory is based upon the temporal and hippocampal structures of speech and memory. This neurological capability allows the subject to revisit the past in search of the image-elements that compose his feeling of self and to turn them into a narrative. On the other, the conscious mind does not have access to our implicit memory, which is simply traced or 'facilitated', as Freud puts it, in the associative cortex around the language zone and on the right side of the brain, which processes time.[80] These pre-verbal experiences imbue the brain with a preferential sensitivity that cannot become conscious, as we do not realize that we have a preferential perception of one type of world: we believe in it because we can see it. This cannot be the repressed, conflict-ridden unconscious described by psychoanalysis. On the other hand, this imprinting, which influences the emotional life of an individual by selecting one type of information, is reminiscent of what Freud calls 'the biological field . . . the underlying bedrock' of the unconscious.[81] The bedrock can suddenly reappear in the form of the samples and ambassadors from the unconscious that emerge in dreams, slips of the tongue or bungled actions.

This argument implies that the non-conscious procedural memory inscribed in our neurones can be reinforced or erased, and that it can, like any biological process, change. We can rework or reshape scripts of self-images by talking about them. When they discover a new archive, historians modify the cultural narratives that tell of social tragedies. Artists transfigure the feelings inspired by a trauma and transform horror into works of art. A close friendship or relationship can change an individual's self-image. By working on our verbal representations, we can rework – from top to bottom in some cases – a self-image or a form of involvement in emotional and social life: 'Narrative is the instrument individuals use to defy destiny.'[82] That is precisely what resilience seeks to do.

We have access to three sources of verbal representations: personal, family and social. A cultural stereotype can be modified by works of art, novels, films or philosophical essays. An environment can be changed by neighbourhood meetings, articles in newspapers or family therapy. We can train ourselves to control the emotions aroused by a fragmented and violent representation by reorganizing and binding together incoherent and unbearable scraps of the traumatic memory. Writing, psychotherapy or a cultural involvement can produce the 'coherent narrative' which will finally produce a clear and peaceful self-image that can at last be accepted by those who are close to us and by our culture.[83]

A Working-Off Mechanism

All resilience tutors are available, provided that the subject's environment and culture do not break them and provided that the wounded subject has acquired a few inner resources that allowed them to be used before his misfortune.

Amédée had always been a very good child. A little too obedient perhaps, given that he was preoccupied with never being late for school, always keeping his homework books neat and tidy and always having his shirt buttoned. Curiously, this conformism desocialized him. Because he was so normal, he became transparent. He did not love his mother and could not get away from her. His adolescence became painfully boring because he was dominated by a woman who took care of everything with such efficiency that, without wishing to, she eclipsed her son and her husband. This went on until Amédée resolved one day to weaken her so as to make himself stronger. One night, when he had to come home late after a boring evening with some friends, he telephoned her, disguised his voice and said: 'Madame B——, this is the hospital. I have to tell you that your son is dead.' Then he hung up and went back to his boring friends. But from that moment on, he felt light-hearted because he could imagine that his mother had at last become vulnerable. He subsequently invented a lot of similar ways of torturing her, and they made him happy. He flirted with suicide, told his mother that he would be having treatment for AIDS when he did not have AIDS, and announced that he was in love with a lorry-driver neighbour his mother loathed. Relationships within the family were becoming oppressive and there were occasional explosions of anger. And then a local newspaper marked the anniversary of the Leclerc army's landing at Juan-les-Pins by publishing an account of how heroic the women had been at liberation. All the neighbours talked to Amédée about the article, and he finally got to know his mother that day. Until then he had never had the opportunity to understand her because he knew her only in her role as a tyrannical servant. He knew nothing about her history because day-to-day life at home had never provided him with the opportunity to realize that his mother was also a person. No one talks to a baby about politics, and daily life had then put the family on a collision course. There was no one in or around Amédée's household to tell him his mother's story. Neither his cousins, his friends nor his neighbours could do so. It was a newspaper which, twenty-five years after the event, played the third-party role by circulating the story he read. From the day he read it, his relationship with his mother was transformed. He became fascinated by the liberation of Provence, read about it, talked to eye-witnesses and then hurried to discuss it with the woman who was his mother. He was discovering her history and her inner world.

Amédée's extreme suffering and the torture he inflicted on his mother merely exacerbated the lack of understanding by repeating the painful relationship. It was an event peripheral to the family – a newspaper article and a cultural narrative – that provoked the change and set the working-through mechanism in motion. This old notion was outlined by a British psychoanalyst as early as 1943. Bibring remarks that the id has a tendency to repeat. It is the traumatic imprint or trace that lingers in the memory that teaches us to see the world through a single prism and to organize it around a single theme. Bibring argues that the ego also has a tendency to restore things to their original state and to re-establish that situation. A return to integrity is an illusory hope, but the psychotrauma can be used for the benefit of the ego and 'to dissolve the tension gradually'.[84] This argument expresses in psychoanalytic terms what neurobiology means when it makes a distinction between implicit memory which, because it is traced in one part of the brain, teaches it to see the world in one particular way, and contrasts it with the explicit memory that produces representations of images and words. Working-through mechanism can be used to rework and reshape the feelings aroused by the real trauma.

Theories of resilience say precisely the same thing. Repetition plays a major role in the construction of our identity because it creates both constants and expectations: 'Whenever I meet that type of man, I always react in the same way. With anger.' Everything that we have learned can fade away with time, or can be reworked by words and images. Thanks to repetition, we get the feeling that we remain ourselves, no matter how much our environment changes, but thanks to resilience we can experience that self-image differently. We can act upon our culture so as to convince it that no wound can justify exclusion, and we can ask society to provide the wounded with a few resilience tutors that will allow them to try to find a new way of developing. 'Working-through mechanisms require the subject to work on himself in depth: the subject must engage in psychical work to overcome the inhibition and to give his creative potential a new dynamism. He has to work at restoring his history in order to see himself as an agent of historicity, and he must transform his relationship with social norms and fight the various forms of power that are the source of humiliating violence.'[85]

The ethical implications of resilience can be summarized as follows: psychical training for new relational skills, work on the history that constitutes our identity, learning to think of ourselves in different ways, and fighting the stereotypes that our culture trots out about the wounded.

IV

The Metaphysics of Love

Filial Tenderness and Romantic Love

'When a sudden surge of sexual desire made me aware of women, I didn't even realize that I'd already learned one way to love. I thought it was them who had changed, but it was me who was seeing them differently. Besides, it was the first time I'd seen women. Before that, I'd seen girls, ladies or mums . . . but not women. I was so confused that I felt feverish. It was like a puzzle, like a sting that was at once stimulating and disturbing, pleasurable and almost a bit painful. I had to understand what was making me so confused. I had to use my body to get one of them to help me learn about the metaphysics of love, about the knowledge that emerges from the world of the senses. I wanted a kind of initiation. A whole bundle of forces was welling up from deep inside me and I looked to family and cultural models for inspiration about how to go about trying to meet a woman I could love.'

'Meeting' and 'love' are both difficult words to come to terms with. Curiously enough, we are proud of them. All the more so in that a great many cultures are now questioning the value of love matches. Arranged marriages are nobler, we are told, because they preserve family structures, provide young couples with support and transmit the values of the group. Whereas you, with your love matches, put the emphasis on individual choice. Communities are weakened when young people neglect collective precepts. Arranged marriages take place inside the group, and that turns them into major social events. In cultures such as this, the first sexual act signals a change of status and is a sort of rite of integration. Whereas a love match brings together two young people who assume they are free to choose one another without really realizing that they are submitting to the social values that inspire them. Which may mean that a love match is a sort of undeclared arranged marriage.

'Meeting' is not a banal word. On the contrary, it is an event, and almost a trauma, because it requires interpenetration. We are disconcerted when we meet someone. If we were not, we would just cross paths or avoid one another. Love is what happens when two people associate their desires in the sexual act and when they combine their emotional styles in their everyday lives. This trauma, which we desire, makes us want to blossom – but with someone else, and there is therefore a danger that we will be burgled. Any encounter can knock us off course and may end in disaster because a man (or woman) who falls in love gives the other the right to enter his (or her) body and soul. The combination of desires and ways of loving gives the loved one the power to make his lover blossom – or tear her apart.

It is only recently that we have looked at the role

attachment plays in love: emotional styles tend to bring two people together because each is a source of comfort to the other and makes him feel so secure that he becomes confident enough – to leave her.[2] First love means renunciation: we have to disobey our Oedipal parental objects,[3] and then rush towards a different sexual object who is willing to play the role of sexual partner. The two processes are of a different nature. We become attached gradually and insidiously in the course of our day-to-day interaction, whereas love seizes hold of our conscious minds. That makes it an event that is as intense as it is disconcerting.

The articulation of the two phenomena is an enigma: how can we reconcile a filial attachment, which forbids sexuality, with romantic love,[4] which is an invitation to sexuality? These two ways of loving are associated, but they are also incompatible, as you cannot love your mother in the way that you love your wife!

We can resolve the problem if we note that when new couples demonstrate their tenderness for each other, they are preparing to have sex. Established couples do not behave in the same way. Tenderness structures an emotional bond that can be dissociated from sexuality because it is a learning process that was inscribed in the implicit memory in the course of interaction between a mother and her baby: we stroke each other's cheeks, snuggle up to each other, hold hands, use 'baby talk', give each other affectionate nicknames, and give each other titbits of food. And then our gestures sometimes get out of hand, change their meaning and synchronize our bodies in preparation for sexual activity. The same sequence of events would be unthinkable with a mother. Just imagining such a scenario is unbearable because it provokes a feeling of horror. We make love on a razor's edge. The extreme proximity of tenderness and desire means that a mere gesture or the slightest physical or verbal signal can turn ecstasy into a nightmare.

Work on attachment now allows us to understand that we learn to love long before we are old enough for sex. Ethological observations help us to analyse how two bodies prepare themselves for this encounter. Then there is the problem of the consequences of this intimacy, which can either put an end to the encounter or modify the way we have woven our attachment. How can we live together after the act of love? How can we reconcile, day after day, our contradictory needs for romantic love and filial tenderness, the desire that sweeps us off our feet and the attachment that keeps us steady?

The Crisis of Love

We now know that emotional styles can be schematically described in terms of secure, ambivalent, avoidant and confused attachments.[5] The ethological method allows us to observe the bodily indices that synchronize the encounter and the way in which emotional styles are adapted to one another. We also know that there is a possibility that bonds that were closely knit might become undone or, on the contrary, that emotional wounds inflicted during childhood might be sutured. It seems logical to see a first love as a major turning point in life, or as the moment when we move from a maternal form of love that keeps us secure to a different form of love in which sexual desire acts as an invitation to an encounter that socializes us. As in any metamorphosis, there is both a contradiction and a continuity between these two ways of loving: a mum is not a dad, but she is not quite a woman either. My wife makes me feel secure because I am attached to her, but she also wants me to desire her. A whole constellation of forces converge as we take this bend: hormones facilitate the creation of new neuronal pathways, an emotional style coordinates the partners, and the social gaze tells us what is and what is not possible.

The raging hormones and emotional intensity of a first love create a real sensitive period, which makes it particularly easy to 'learn' our partner. The biological basis for this imprinting is neurohormonal. When human beings feel no stress because they are so secure as to become numb, their environment becomes undifferentiated. They have no way of marking the passage of time, and cannot construct any identity. Conversely, too much stress affects the very anatomy of the brain. When life is difficult, the organism is flooded with catecholamine neurotransmitters and the adrenal glands secrete cortisol. These substances are preferentially taken up by the limbic cells in the lower part of the brain. The cortisol causes an oedema in the wall which, when it swells up, dilates the neural pathways. Calcium ions flood in and cause the cell to burst. This explains why the brain's limbic system, which controls the emotions and the memory, is often atrophied after a few years of daily stress.[6]

The healthy stimulation of the brain must therefore avoid both the complete security that deadens the emotional life, and the extreme stress that paralyses psychical life by atrophying the circuits of the emotions and memory. Like the in-and-out rhythm of the beating of the heart and of breathing, it is the alternating rhythm that makes us feel alive. This explains why, in physiological terms, we are forced to seek out ordeals in order to overcome them. We therefore set ourselves artificial existential milestones that make us feel euphoric, even though they are difficult to achieve. When it is aroused by a manageable level of stress, the organism secretes oxytocin, a mood-elevating substance that is found in large quantities after sex, pregnancy, breast-feeding or the announcement of good news. More of the small morphine-like molecules known as opioids are also produced after a pleasant discussion, spending time in good company or listening to music.[7]

In that sense, the crisis of love brings together and coordinates all these biological, emotional and social factors. It creates a sensitive period that is so intense that we can 'learn' the other and incorporate him or her into our memories, but there is also a danger that we will suffer a traumatic wound. That is why, when a lover says, 'I can't think about anything but her,' he is actually talking about himself: his image of her fills his entire inner world.

A Pre-Verbal Declaration of Love

'I immediately felt that we were in love . . . No . . . I immediately felt that we could let love grow. I was just about to walk out of the bookshop when she caught my eye. And I do mean "caught". I was caught, almost possessed. She seized hold of me and I was delighted. She was sitting in the middle of a group of tourists who were browsing through the art books. She watched me leave. I realized in a flash that I had made something happen for her. She was beautiful and her gentle beauty penetrated me deeply. We understood each other. So I wrapped her gaze in mine. It was both gentle and intense. When we looked at each other, I experienced something like a dangerous pleasure, a pleasure that bordered on anxiety. I nodded my head to say "Goodbye". I couldn't stop myself. But the emotional intensity that little word made me feel was a big event for me. She mumbled something that probably meant "Hello". She was serious, and I could tell that her voice was shaking. Her group of friends signalled that it was time to go. She looked away, looked back at me sadly and went away. That's how our love story ended.'

This adventure, which lasted for no longer than it took to exchange glances, illustrates the problem of how we meet someone we love: how could this verbal message be so clear? Why her? Why this delicious feeling that is so close to being a trauma? What would we have been like as a couple if we had connected after falling in love at first sight?

Our courtship displays are primarily non-verbal. Like all living creatures, we have to synchronize our emotions and adjust our bodies long before we mate. We have succeeded in convincing ourselves that it is what we say that allows us to meet our partners. Unfortunately, the ethology of conversation proves that, even in the most intellectual of exchanges, much of what we have to say is communicated by our bodies, and without us knowing it. If we blocked our paraverbal exchanges by doing away with postures, gestures, facial expressions and verbal hesitations, we would not be able to understand a thing, as what our words transmit represents scarcely 35 per cent of the message.[8]

If we accept the idea that we speak in order to affect others in such a way as to make them receptive to our emotions, we can understand why we can fall in love at first sight. Take the example of the lightning exchange that occurred as the man and woman left the bookshop. The body of one partner transmitted a pre-verbal message to the other. If they had been able to speak to each other, they might have pursued this emotional exchange and might have confirmed that they really were in love. The text is of little importance. It is the co-text that matters and the sensed proximity of their bodies might have continued the emotional bonding that began when they first set eyes on each other.

Despite what our stereotypes say, it is almost always the woman who triggers the human male's courtship display.[9] Women send out signals to say that they are interested and available. We know the intensity of their gaze when we see it, but it is hard to define. Men rarely approach women uninvited, with the exception of rapists or men who, because of their disordered emotional development, have not learned the empathy that would otherwise allow them to harmonize their desires. It is not so much the canons of beauty that trigger love as women's talent for triggering emotions. Men have probably acquired the same relational skills, but the signals appear to be gender-specific.

A man suffering from a manic-depressive disorder will conquer the hearts of many women during his euphoric phases. But when he is in his melancholic phase and when his world is a lonely place because he is empty, the same man will not notice the signals sent out by a woman who is interested in him. It has to be added that our emotional development helps to determine the meaning we attribute to the signals we perceive. Many women who, as girls, learned to love a sad parent in a solemn way are exasperated by the cheerful behaviour of euphoric or smooth-talking, self-confident men. When they run away from such men or simply avoid them, they are taking shelter from the lightning that might strike women who seek out cheerful men who can make them laugh. The signals are clearly perceived in both cases, but they take on a different meaning, depending upon the emotional development of the woman in question: most securely attached women send out signals of interest to men who are cheerful and self-confident, whereas avoidant women will become tense and give the same men icy looks.

Lightning does not strike at random, and it strikes only the rods that were constructed when we were learning our various emotional styles as children. We have already invented all our future partners, which is why the chance event that leads us to meet someone will occur within a limited range of possibilities. We never fall in love with just anyone. We always meet the corresponding object for whom we have been shaped, and no one else. We are all both receivers and actors who can find the man or woman with whom we can communicate. We are struck by each other because we have the ability to affect each other.

When marriages are arranged, their determinants are clearly stated by culture, religion, race or money. But in the case of a love match, emotional signals come to the fore, whilst social pressures are at work behind the scenes. When a woman is bowled over because a man she does not know touches something deep inside her, she tries to calm her emotions. She makes a lot of little gestures directed towards herself: she tugs at her skirt, pats her hair, lifts her chin, pushes her breasts out and tries not to smile. Although she is touching herself, she is also sending out inviting signals. She does not realize that she is giving the man stealthy glances, raising her eyebrows, creasing up her eyes, and putting her hand in front of her mouth.[10] She does not know it, but her aroused body is tracing a geometric shape that lets the man know that she would be only too happy if he began to talk to her. He feels that and knows that, but he does not know how he knows. Ethological observation is the only thing that could explain to him that the emotion he has inspired is being expressed in the form of a powerful invitation: her dilated pupils give her gaze a warmth that he can perceive quite clearly. Because they are more sensitive to images, males perceive bodily indices and respond to them by making behavioural and verbal approaches, whilst women, who are more sensitive to touch, experience a man's first words as a verbal caress.

When a man's pupils began to dilate, a woman takes no notice, but his first words and the manner in which he speaks are,[11] for her, an emotional sample of what is to come. At this point in the encounter, how he speaks is more important than what he says. The speech act maintains the proximity that allows all the other forms of sensorial activity that begin to match their personalities. The woman is usually the first to establish physical contact, but she only touches socially permissible parts of his body. As she is talking to him, she will casually brush his forearm with the tips of her fingers. When he says goodbye, she lets her hand linger in his. When they meet again, she will flick dust off his jacket with what appears to be nothing more than a minor maternal gesture. She will let her dress brush against him and, in a crowded room, her breasts will accidentally press against the arm of her suitor as he is pushed by the crowd. All these little touches mean that she is letting the man know that she would like him to touch her elsewhere and to touch parts of her body that are, in social terms, less permissible but also more intimate.

Meeting a new lover is not as accidental as it might seem. The only thing accidental about it is the choice of a very small number of signifiers. It is as though people who are falling in love are saying: 'There is something about the man (woman) I have just met that speaks to my soul. His (her) body shows indices that touch me deep inside because my history has sensitized me to them, and because he (she) can talk to me more easily than to others.'

First Love, Second Chance

The first stages of our adaptation to love consist of bodily indices that reveal emotional styles which have already been learned. Ethological observations are beginning to explain how insidious attachments play a role in momentary infatuations.

The intensity of the moment we fall in love and the interpenetration of emotional styles create a sensitive period in which a reactivated learning process allows both partners to blossom by giving them the pleasures of discovery. It becomes possible to correct what may previously have been a difficult emotional style. But the same sensitive period can also make a poorly woven emotional style worse or even tear apart what was a secure attachment.

This really is a sensitive period in which other learning processes can get under way. It is one of life's turning points and often triggers a resilience process but, conversely, it can also damage a partner whose attachment was closely woven. The force that determines which direction the relationship will take is a combination of emotional styles and a set of historical and para-verbal forces. They determine how the couple are with each other. The way they are matched can facilitate an emotional reworking in which each partner influences the other, either for better or for worse. The security of being in a relationship can help both partners to learn the secure attachment they previously failed to acquire. This explains why love makes resilience possible. In biological terms, a loving relationship also facilitates metamorphoses and changes of direction. The emotional intensity and the hormonal secretions have an effect on the brain that corresponds to a new synaptogenesis. New and previously unwired neural pathways are established.[12] All these conditions combine to facilitate a new imprinting. Young people are still marked by the early environment that taught them their emotional style, and a loving relationship gives them a second chance by allowing them to modify the negative self-images they acquired in childhood.[13] It can even allow them to cease being delinquents and to commit themselves to a new style of socialization.[14]

This is much more than a transition. It really is one of life's turning points, and sometimes even a metamorphosis in which the biological, the emotional and the social combine to take the corner with various degrees of success.

Any theory of resilience, therefore, has to look at the changes we have observed and at the effective and cultural conditions that modify the organism's receptiveness. By creating new sensitive periods, the subject undergoes a new imprinting that modifies his or her emotional style. These turning points allow the subject to acquire unexpected relational skills and a new way of savouring the world. Our emotional style means that we are likely to meet a particular kind of partner, and that in turn modifies our emotional style.

The survey method of sending out questionnaires to which subjects can, should they wish, reply anonymously gives us an overview of sexual encounters in the population at large.[15] One such survey found that 16 per cent of those under twenty-four and 22 per cent of those over fifty had had no sexual relations in the previous year; 70 per cent of those over sixty-five were no longer sexually active; and 2.7 per cent of men and 1.7 per cent of women had had several homosexual encounters. If we attempt to correlate attachment and sexuality, the interesting point is that the unmarried had a lot of sexual encounters, which is quite understandable, but also that intellectuals whose relationships with their partners were less intensely physical had a greater number of extra-marital affairs. An existential style can therefore influence the way we organize our sex lives. The arrows dispatched by Cupid do not strike at random. Love's little archers aim only at the men and women who set themselves up as targets. The random element only affects those who put themselves in the firing line and who do not jump out of the way. 'How we met', or the couple's foundation myth,[16] becomes the organizational principle behind the couple's characteristic personality, relational style and commitment. In arranged marriages, what is expected of a couple is clearly stated by their culture and young people are proud to submit to the law of the group. In love matches, in contrast, the decision to live together is more psychological; social pressures, although very powerful, become more personal. Freedom to choose a love partner expands the circle of potential partners, and less notice is taken of social constraints.

Embers of Affection in a Cold Family

For years, Georges was astonished by the intense but gentle emotion he had felt when, as a young boy, he saw a father fussing over his little boy. He often replayed the scene in his mind because it gave him so much pleasure. He had been out skiing one day. It was very foggy and he stopped at the top of a steep path to catch his breath for a moment. Below him he saw a man who was obviously a father, even though he could not see him very well against the greyish white of the mist and the white snow. The man was tying his little boy's muffler. He then set off on his skis again and slowly disappeared, followed by the child. He was a big man, and 'big' was the important word, as it was that which gave Georges the pleasure he experienced. The father had devoted a little of his brute strength to a tender relationship with his little boy. Subsequently, Georges often went to look for this image in his memory, and he was always surprised at how much pleasure it afforded him.

He had spent his childhood in a cold family in which no one ever said anything. His father took every opportunity to disappear. His silent and over-worked mother would rebuff Georges with a gesture of annoyance whenever he tried to go near her. His little sister broke everything she could lay her hands on and kept running away from home from morning to night. The family's days were spent in a sullen silence. The little girl was an expert on avoidant attachment. She put up with her mother's physical roughness, and never protested when she gave her a shove to indicate what she wanted her to do without ever saying a word to her. In self-defence, she prevented herself from loving her and, being convinced that she could not depend on others, taught herself not to cry. She walled herself up in a closed world, and came out of it only to run away.

Living in this leaden atmosphere, Georges relished the few moments of emotional warmth he could find outside the house. When he was out shopping, he used to have long chats with the greengrocer and used to take an old lady her bread and milk because she had trouble climbing four flights of stairs at her age. He dreamed that, when he was grown up, he would start a family where they would talk a lot and laugh together. As an adolescent, he had a fantasy about crawling into a sleeping bag where a woman was waiting for him. Simply being there side by side with her in the warmth of the bag was enough to make him happy. For the first two years of his life, his parents had placed him with a very cheerful child-minder. In her company he blossomed, and the secure attachment-style that he had been taught by that pleasurable encounter was probably imprinted on his memory. When his little sister came along, his mother stayed at home to look after her two children and kept Georges with her. Day-to-day life began to feel very chilly. But the boy who could still remember what a happy relationship felt like would go to see his old neighbour or the greengrocer when he wanted a few moments of emotional warmth. The mere presence of girls made him feel happy, which may explain the sleeping bag fantasy. He found sexuality disturbing because there was a danger that any family of his own might also be silent and oppressive. He said to himself quite clearly – and more than once – that if some girl were to have his baby he would never leave her, even if they were unhappy together. Investing so much in a personal commitment frightened him and he found it easier to avoid all sexual activity because he experienced it as something dangerous. The girls liked him a lot because he was a good-looking boy who happily chatted away to them and did not pester them or make any sexual advances. Some of them actually thought that he did not pester them enough because he remained just a friend and did not respond to the signals of female sexual invitation that they were sending out.

And then, on a snowy ski slope, Georges fell in love at first sight. There was no element of sexuality involved, but there was something profoundly emotional about seeing a hefty man fussing over his little boy. 'So you can be that kind of father. That's what I've been dreaming of.' A random encounter had allowed him to witness a scene that acted out the theme of his emotional life: 'Sexuality means something now and it's no longer frightening, provided that some woman lets me become that kind of father.' Georges had grown up in a cold family but had also known a few embers of affection, and the combination of the two had made him eager to witness a parental scene that would have reduced most boys of his age to tears of laughter.

What Werther experienced when he fell in love with Charlotte at first sight was also asexual. The young man fell in love with her when he saw her cutting some bread for her brothers and sisters. He 'beheld the most charming scene I have ever set eyes on . . . She was holding a loaf of rye bread and cutting a piece for each of the little ones around her'.[17] Werther, like Georges, saw something in the real world that corresponded to what he wanted so badly. For him, this scene was an event that touched him deeply, whereas his friends would have laughed at it.

All that remains to be done now is to make a baby. How to introduce a spermatozoid to an ovule is the only problem. But once it has been born, the child will have to grow up inside a sensory environment as it is touched, cradled, fed, cleaned and caressed with words. This time, it is the meeting between two emotional styles and the combination of different parental ways of loving that are problematic.

The Alchemy of Ways of Loving

When a couple get together, they must both desire one another and become attached to one another. Now, as a child develops, the two ways of loving become dissociated and may even come into conflict because the only way an adolescent can feel at ease is by desiring someone outside his family of origin. When a young man becomes a parent, the sensorial field that provides his child with its development tutors consists of a combination of parental emotional styles. Some combinations pose a threat to the identity of one partner, whilst others allow what was a badly woven bond to begin to evolve further.[18]

Suppose Mr Secure marries Miss Secure. The bond between them will be light, which does not mean that it is superficial. They will love each other dearly, and perhaps deeply, but the bond will be light because, as children, they both acquired the ability to trust others deeply. This gives them the pleasure of discovering and of loving one another as they are. Couples like this share their daily lives quite happily, spend short periods apart and then happily meet up and tell each other about their respective social adventures.

Mr Distress is unlikely to meet Miss Distress as neither of them will put themselves in the way of Cupid's arrow. They are handicapped by their suffering. If they stayed together, they would quarrel all the time because that would allow them to put up with the present without dreaming about the future. Miss Distress might, on the other hand, meet Mr Ambivalent, who has learned to want to make reparation to a woman. It is possible that Mr Fear-of-losing will meet Miss I-enjoy-life and that their arrangement will allow them to change: her stable but gloomy presence is enough to make him feel secure, and he can therefore energize her. Relationships can be based on many different combinations of ways of loving.

Laurent loved his mother a great deal but he was ashamed of her. She was poor, old and badly dressed, and her apron was always wet. When she came to pick him up from school, he asked her to keep away from the other mums, who were young and pretty. Yet he liked to cuddle up to her and dreamed that he would make her happy one day. He missed her when she wasn't there but rejected her so as not to have to compare her with the other mothers. When he was old enough to embark on a relationship, Laurent still displayed the ambivalence he had acquired as a child. When he met a woman who loved him, he rejected her and then rediscovered that he needed her permanent emotional presence to keep him stable. So he asked her to come back. The day he thought he had lost her, he asked her to marry him. She did not enjoy life, was frightened of going out and experienced every friendly encounter as a dreadful ordeal. She was afraid of life and he was afraid of losing her, so they enjoyed a stable relationship. In order to ward off her fear of life, he dealt with their social problems. She warded off his fear of being left alone by letting him know that she would always be there. Because they could support each other, they did well at university and had four children. She looked after them very well because they gave her the perfect alibi for avoiding all social encounters. Because he could take advantage of the emotional security his wife guaranteed him, he gradually – and late in life – acquired the trusting attachment his unfortunate mother had been unable to give him. When he had finally gained a sense of security and had been cured by his wife, he decided to leave her.

Relationships in which one partner acts as the other's therapist are not uncommon. They deserve respect, provided that the partners can renegotiate their contract. They need to do so because, if by some mischance they were happy together, they would no longer have any reason to go on living together. Laurent's inner resources were modified and strengthened by his wife's permanent emotional presence. Thanks to her, he acquired the secure attachment that allowed him to love another woman differently. Thanks to him she learned to avoid her fear of social life, but she did not learn to overcome it. If he had not been such a kind husband, had taken less interest in her and had solved fewer of their day-to-day problems, Laurent might have allowed his wife to learn to be sociable and the couple might have renegotiated their contract by establishing a lighter bond.

A first love is a second chance, and a second love is a third chance. Subsequent loves are disasters because we do not have enough time to start learning again.

Both ecological reality and biological reality are constantly evolving. The feelings aroused by representations of images or words also change, but we can act upon them by making films, painting, putting on plays and thinking and talking in such a way as to work upon and modify them. This is what makes resilience possible. Psychoanalysis refers to resilience in a relational convention that we can extend to other domains of life: '[. . .] recalling previously inaccessible episodes so as to allow memories to be "resolved": this work makes it possible to reduce the emotional tension, to prevent the repetition of inadequate responses and to encourage the development of new responses . . .'[19] Attachment theory has two further contributions to make to the psychoanalytic solution. It stresses that memory, like anything that is biological, can be modified, and adds that we can work upon the subjective and social representations that we carry around with us.

A couple's emotional styles marry when they first meet because, on seeing the other, each partner expects him or her to satisfy a need or wish: 'the mnemonic image [of a certain perception] remains associated . . . with the memory trace of the excitation produced by the need. As a result of the link that has just been established, next time this need arises a psychical impulse will at once emerge which will seek to recathect the mnemonic image of the perception [. . .] the reappearance of the perception is the fulfilment of the wish.'[20]

We can also say: 'What I perceive in the other reawakens traces of my past and triggers my need to rediscover them. I am committing myself to this relationship, together with both my dreams for the future and the scores I have to settle. With this capital of memories, emotions and desires, we will sign the implicit contract that provides the themes of our family life.'

When Mr Frigid met Miss Afraid-of-sex, they both immediately saw the behavioural indices that allowed them to hope that their inner worlds could be coordinated. Their alliance reinforced the emotional lessons they had learned because each of them could see that the other was sending out the behavioural signals they wanted to see.[21] They married, enjoyed a stable relationship and were not happy. They had only one child, who was conceived during one of their rare and joyless sexual encounters.

The alchemy of emotional styles is not always as sad as this, and it is actually possible to gain something from an expensive contract, as we can see from the story of Mr Pegleg and Miss Afraid-of-everything. He lost his leg during the war and her phobia transformed his handicap into a gain. As he had difficulty in walking, she resolved to devote herself to her husband's handicap – and let everyone around her know it. She took his arm when he stumbled, made sure he had his hat on because he could not stand the sun, and brought him the daily glass of orange juice that prevented him from dying before the evening was out. She had her groceries delivered to the house and ordered everything by phone because the slightest absence would have snuffed out Mr Pegleg's candle. We greatly admired this woman, and the local priest said that she might even be made a saint. Because her husband was protected in this way, he not only survived but, because there was nothing else to distract him, worked all the time and did very well in life. Until the day that Miss Afraid-of-everything died of an embolism. Her husband would surely join her in the grave; a candle flame is easily blown out – you must be joking! He was plunged deep into grief, and to help himself get over his sorrow he bought a car and began to travel the world. Without a hat and without his orange juice!

Sometimes, the alliance works to the advantage of one partner only when things are going badly. Mr On-and-off loved Miss Near-him dearly but could not understand what he called her 'power cuts'. The electrical metaphor came to him because he was a chemist and because it was perfectly clear to him: either they loved each other, or they did not. It was either on or off. Unfortunately, the electricity was only on when the lady was anxious. Fortunately, she often had bouts of anxiety and could find no relief unless she was with him. She would throw her arms around his neck and hug him, just as she had learned to do with her mother. But if he approached her when she had calmed down, she resented him as an intruder and sent him packing. She only loved him when she was not well. Which is why, during a long period of remission, she asked him for a divorce and was then reduced to despair because she could no longer be with him.

Miss Me-first married Mr Her-first and everyone thought they were the perfect couple until the day he made a tragic slip of the tongue. Insisting that there were no problems in their relationship, he said: 'My wife and I respect each other. She does whatever she likes. And I do whatever she likes.' The involuntary revelation was followed by a long silence.

Mr Her-first tried to pay his wife less attention but could not succeed in doing so because the emotional style he had acquired as a child was so devoid of hope that he had concluded that he could be in a relationship only if he could take over the life of the woman he loved. Although it was terribly expensive, this emotional style was very profitable because it slowly taught him to love in the lighter way typical of a secure attachment.

Emotional change is, then, possible. The emotional style we acquired as children is a tendency that will orient our subsequent relationships, but it is not a destiny that petrifies love. A loving couple – the smallest possible family-group system – is a place for interactions and, when the time is right, we can rework what we have learned. 'A relational style is not the sum total of each partner's attachments. It is something they build together. It is their creation.'[22] A loving couple share what they discover, and either benefit from it or suffer because of it.

Verbal Mating

Secure couples have a characteristic style of interaction. It demonstrates that the inevitable tensions of life can be resolved thanks to their 'goal-adjusted partnership'[23] and 'reflexive consciousness',[24] which is another way of saying that the couple talk to each other to explain themselves and cooperate in order to achieve their goals.

We can observe this way of talking. Secure couples take it in turns to speak because they pay as much attention to each other's bodies as to their words, listen to what each partner is saying and watch them speak. They readily perceive the bodily index, the accelerated speech, the lowered voice and the sudden glance at the listener that indicates that the speaker is about to let him or her speak. This behavioural-verbal dance demonstrates that the couple have harmonized their emotions and are looking for a peaceful solution. In contrast, insecure and preoccupied couples, who have signed an implicit care-contract, display great psycho-motor instability as they chat to each other: the unstoppable flow of words, the abrupt changes of subject, the failure to get to the point, and the self-centred behaviours directed at external objects have nothing to do with the conversation. They are responses to feelings triggered in them by the other and the partners are not acting in harmony. They interrupt each other because they are afraid of being dominated, or simply because they take no account of the inner world the other is trying to express.

Some insecure-avoidant subjects seem to be so detached that their bodies become rigid; they make few gestures, use short sentences and speak coldly without any verbal music or facial expressions. Their exaggerated self-control reveals an emotional numbness that often makes their interlocutor feel overwhelmed.

The imprecise words used by attachment-disordered subjects, the evasive answers they give and their inappropriate gestures make it difficult to understand what they are saying and this exacerbates their isolation and distress.[25]

The way people speak reveals their inner world and makes it possible to observe how partners adjust to one another. We can:

- Observe emotional styles that were acquired before we met our partners;
- Understand what young people imagine love to be;
- Analyse how the signifiers we see on the other's body allow us to meet the one we love;
- Calculate the alchemy of a couple's interactions, which never add up to make $1 + 1 = 2$. In a fusional couple $1 + 1 = 1$. In a secure couple $1 + 1 = 2 + 2$. In a one-sided couple where one partner eats the other, $1 + 1 = 2 + 0$.

Time to Learn to Love

Given that we know how to observe how each partner becomes imprinted on and modifies the other, we can also state that couples who are in love sign an implicit contract. It is easier to sign the contract than to get out of it. Are we repeating a way of loving? Does it so happen that we cannot bear to be apart from someone we cannot live with? Can we care for each other? Can we be traumatized by love? Or can we demonstrate that we have become resilient?

In most cases, love improves emotional styles. Many subjects with ambivalent or avoidant attachments improve their level of serenity and develop secure attachments. Of course, the story is not always idyllic.

Perhaps Miss No-one-loves-me will meet Mr Me-first. She will be so bowled over by her partner's love that she will do whatever he wants so as to keep him for a while. Mr Me-first will offer Miss No-one-loves-me a 'Me-first' contract, and she will be only too eager to sign it. And everyone will be amazed by the stable relationship between such a virile man and such a gentle woman.

Therapeutic agreements in which each partner asks the other to take care of him or her are not unusual either. They are double-edged as they can both cure people and tear them apart. When Miss Alone-in-the-world discovered that Mr No-emotions was available, she ran to help him. They helped each other a lot because they made each other feel secure, and both their day-to-day lives and their way of loving visibly improved. The only problem was that they could not bear to be apart because they were so dependent on each other, and one could easily imagine that, if one of them fell ill, he or she would criticize the other for not taking care of them.

I knew Mr Oh-I-hate-you well. He married Miss Don't-give-a-damn and their relationship made a curious impression on me. She would talk about her health, her few pleasures and about how unhappy she was. Her husband listened in silence, his tight-lipped facial expressions and looks of exasperation clearly indicating that he was annoyed, even though he said nothing. He followed her everywhere she went and when his wife was excluded from the conversation for some reason, he asked her questions that would get her talking about the dress she was wearing or about how well she had slept last night. He felt abandoned when she was not there, and dominated when she was there. So, he would seek her out, give her power and then rebel against her. This little scenario could be observed in all their conversations. They were chained to each other, and their way of being together allowed them both to love one another and to complain about it.

In a small number of cases, passion triggers a real trauma because people in love can be overcome by intolerable emotions. The dividing line between love and trauma is often a fine one because we are talking about a critical period in which the subject's personality can be reshaped. Most of the time, the corner is taken safely but accidents do happen when the emotional intensity tears apart a fragile personality that has suffered a delightful shock.

'Love that doesn't hurt isn't real love,' Ginette explained to me. 'This way of loving makes me unhappy, but if I love gently, I can't tell if I'm in love or not. A pedestrian love affair would leave me disappointed. A passion that tears me apart is the only thing that can prove to me that I am in love and at the same time it hurts to be in love.' In her day-to-day life, Ginette always required proof. A painful passion gave her the cruel and reassuring proof she needed. 'Love makes me think of my early childhood, when I used to cling to my mother: I was madly in love when I was in contact with her and in despair whenever she went away. I feel nostalgic for that suffering. It gave me all the love I needed and made me feel safe. That's the way I like to love.' The adult Ginette's need for a painful passion showed that she had learned to love in an ambivalent way. She loved her partner in the same way that you love the bed of nails you cling to because you are afraid of drowning.

I followed up a small population of adolescents with emotional disorders and tried to assess their attachment style when they were with their parents, and then after their first experience of love.[26] On the whole, these young people, whose emotional development had been difficult, improved after their first experience of love. Despite their difficulties, they learned to love more happily and more lightly. There was a significant rise in their secure-attachment indices. They discovered the pleasures of chatting, being trusted, accepting the influence of those they loved, making projects, talking about their past and inventing a few of the rituals that allow couples to weave their intimacy.[27]

The moment we fall in love is a wonderful turning point. It is also dangerous because some secure attachments and rather more insecure attachments fail to take the bend and crash. But those who do succeed in negotiating the bend improve as a result.

Suffering the Pain of Those We Love

When someone who is in love attempts to take his bend, his or her family takes it with him. This is another way of saying that the family is as involved as he or she is in both the joy and the trauma. When the bombs went off at the Port-Royal RER station in Paris on 3 December 1996, some of those caught up in the explosion were not traumatized, and instead it was their partners who suffered the serious post-traumatic stress syndrome.[28] The same phenomenon had already been observed during the war in Vietnam, where the twin who had not seen combat suffered more than the twin who had. Similarly, UN soldiers in Beirut suffered more than the fighters. Some children whose parents were deported to camps in Germany during the Second World War were even more badly affected than their parents. It is therefore not the traumatic event that is transmitted and that damages the close relative, but its representation. In some cases, someone who is injured but has a lot of support can recover from the trauma more easily than the close relative who was thought to be protected, and who was left to face the horrors of what he imagined. Before we can suffer from our idea of what our loved ones are suffering, we must, however, be able to put ourselves in their place. We find ourselves in the same situation as Mr Her-first, who could only feel right when he had done everything he could to make his wife feel right. Myrna Gannagé's work is influenced by ideas of Melanie Klein and René Spitz's ethological method, and observations of children who were traumatized by the wartime air raids on London. She found that, during the war in Lebanon, children whose parents were traumatized were more affected than children whose parents survived unscathed. Even the orphans, who either banded together or were placed with peaceful families, were better protected than the children who stayed with their traumatized families.[29] It is the whole family unit that suffers or pulls through, that either survives the psychotrauma or is over-whelmed by it. When someone is hurt, there is a 27 per cent possibility that his or her family will suffer because of what he or she has suffered. When a child dies, one in two couples separate within a year. Women who are raped often ask for a separation, even though their husbands were not to blame for what happened to them.[30]

Sandra was a bodyguard. She liked a fight and, having trained to perfection, was famous for her accuracy with a revolver. After having acted as an important man's escort one night, she decided to walk home. A man followed her, caught up with her and raped her in a doorway. He was stronger than her and she could not even draw her gun. She eventually staggered home after wandering the streets in a daze for some time. Her partner had been waiting up for her and told her he'd been worried about her because she was so late. She exploded, screamed that she hated men and threw out the man she had been living with so contentedly. Reduced to despair by the loneliness she had created, she called her mother, who came running and sank into the same depression. The two women have still not recovered.

Odette went on a cruise with her husband. When the ship put in at a little port on the Turkish coast, she went for a walk by herself. Two men grabbed her and laughed as they raped her. She ran to take refuge in the arms of her husband who, without saying a word, went to the police station and then went to look for her attackers. When the ship left port, the behaviour of her unusually silent husband showed that he still cared about his injured wife. Their sadness disappeared within a few months.

Sandra's self-image was all the more badly damaged because she had not been able to fight back or draw her gun. 'I'm only a woman,' she kept repeating. Before she was attacked, she had had no difficulty in proving that she was capable of doing her job.

As she made her way back to the cruise ship, the humiliated and morally wounded Odette thought to herself: 'My husband won't want to have anything to do with a woman who has been defiled.' But she discovered him to be a resolute man who shared her distress and then gave her his support by behaving affectionately towards her.

Both women suffered serious assaults, but their subsequent evolution depended upon their families. Sandra's family did not survive the disaster, whereas Odette's husband was able to repair some of the damage. Both situations forced their families to change. But whereas Sandra's pain made her family system become introverted, Odette's became more open and thus demonstrated the solidity of a couple who were trying to fight adversity.

Understanding and Nursing Are Two Different Things

Just as a family can lessen the pain of one of its members, a culture can also give it very different meanings. Psychotraumas are rare in societies where shamans still have a role to play, as they do in Siberia. Real life is very harsh and teaches some cruel lessons, but as soon as one of its members is hurt, the group, orchestrated by the shaman, rallies around and uses magical rituals to reintegrate him. The rituals are a way of controlling adversity by using song, dance, make-up and spells to drive out the evil spirits and to allow the injured to retake possession of an inner world that has been shattered by the accident. The trauma occurred in the real world and inflicted a serious wound, but the psychotrauma did not have time to develop because the wound was immediately bandaged by the group and integrated into its cultural mythology.

Something similar happened in the United States after the terrorist attacks of 11 September 2001. New Yorkers were not renowned for their kindheartedness: 'If someone collapses in the street, they step over him so as not to be late in getting to the office' was the stereotype. The incredible horror of seeing the twin towers collapse in flames instantly produced a solidarity reflex: families, friends and even strangers rushed to help New Yorkers in their time of need. No one had ever seen so many restaurant owners setting up tables in the street so that the rescue workers could rest and eat for free before throwing themselves back into the fray. The whole world tried to understand what had happened and to draw up projects to defend itself . . . or to strike back. In real terms, 11 September was a huge blow, but the culture of New York changed in the years that followed the atrocity: people began to talk to each other, to invite each other home and to help one another. The suicide rate was at its lowest since 1930! Siberian shamans and New York restaurant owners allow us to understand the extent to which cultures become involved in traumas.

Our children have never been so well looked after. We have never had a better understanding of their inner worlds, and yet they are more depressed and anxious than ever. Everyone finds this amazing. We simply have to accept that understanding and nursing are two different things, and that there is always a price to be paid for progress. The technology that allows us to remove ourselves from the physical world is a recent invention. Before it came along, our bodies were the main tools we used to change the world, and they were more efficient than machines. Men physically produced society by going down the mines, and women, many of whom were already working in the fields and factories, perpetuated that culture by producing the workers, peasants and princesses of the future. Those who control the machines now control the world, and the victory they have won has had the effect of creating a virtual humanity with a very impoverished emotional world. In the Middle Ages, we lived in a world of representations that made it easy to accept the death of children and frequent famines. Thanks to the technological advances we have made, we now have more control over the real world, but men's labour is no longer an offering to their wives, who make their own living. And women are less likely to play their role in keeping families together because they are no longer prepared to sacrifice themselves. Progress does give us more control over blows inflicted on us by reality and does allow our personalities to blossom, whatever our gender. It also has its side effects: as the standard of living improves, social bonds become looser because we no longer need each other in order to survive and develop. Technical and cultural progress spares us a lot of real traumas but, when disaster does strike, we have no control over its psychic effects because progress has done away with the shaman-effect.

The other side effect of this personal development is the destruction of parental roles. The wage system and the undeniable progress we have made give men a lot of material comforts, and they give women a great deal of freedom. Surveys carried out in Sweden, where social stratification tends not to be based upon a hierarchy of skills (experts at the top, and the unskilled at the bottom), found that men do well in the private sector, whereas women are better socialized in stable wage-earning structures such as the national health service and in public institutions.[31] This is another way of saying that, when traumas do occur, the wage system that makes men both secure and numb affords women better protection and that state involvement in their emancipation modifies and sexualizes resilience-tutors.

The way marital and parental roles have changed over the last thirty years has completely altered the family structure in which our children grow up. Their sensorial world and their daily rhythms are no longer what they once were, nor is parental involvement. Fifty years ago, little girls came into the world to help their families, and little boys were destined to become their parents' 'walking sticks' in a society in which there were no old-age pensions. We no longer talk about babies in that way, and filiation has therefore undergone a metamorphosis. Children are no longer descended from their parents. It is the children who run the household, who set the rhythm for outings and holidays and who decide when their families should move house. The growing instability of these new family structures is creating multiple attachment systems, which sometimes work to the advantage of children because they allow them to escape from tyrannical or psychologically damaged parents. This also means that there are more adults around them, and their fleeting attachment to those adults does not allow them to experience any emotional serenity.

The future of this way of loving is uncertain. Social groups, families and individuals who think that personal fulfilment should take priority defend these emotional styles. Those who find autonomy a daunting prospect are discovering the virtues of 'modern-style' arranged marriages in which adults offer their young people a limited number of choices. They are allowed to meet a few suitors from within their religious, social or racial group so as to preserve their feeling of belonging. The inter-generational bond is strengthened by respect for the elderly, acceptance of their values and the emotional and material help they receive in return.

How we choose between these relational strategies depends upon the social context in which we find ourselves. When autonomy is difficult, belonging to a group has a reassuring effect. It tells us which path we should follow and which set of potential sexual partners we can choose from. But when the social context improves, when it is easy to find work and housing and when morality is tolerant, the weight of parental authority becomes an obstacle to young people's pursuit of happiness. This paradox is not a contradiction because we have learned that parental affection provides the secure base that gives young people the strength to leave the family cocoon. In a comfortable social context, conflict offers hope of liberation.[32] In a difficult society, we happily surrender to the family group. We take refuge in it. It makes us feel secure and acts as our tutor. But in a tolerant civilization, the family that gives young people the strength to leave becomes a hindrance if it cannot hand them over to a community that welcomes them.

V

Inheriting Hell

Memory and Guilt

What we pass on to our children probably depends upon a whole range of forces, both good and evil. They learn about them without the knowledge of their partners and internalize them without realizing it. That something should be transmitted is inevitable, as we cannot love other people and live alongside them without passing on something. How does this transmission work, and what does it change in the inner world of our partners? That is the enigma. It is easy to find lots of children and grandchildren whose parents and grandparents were traumatized. If we look at the evolution of these damaged parents and then at that of their children, we can try to shed some light on the problem.

There are now 200,000 survivors of the Nazi persecutions living in Israel. They were very young at the time of the Holocaust, but it can be assumed that they have been living for the last fifty years with the immense wound that was inflicted on them. Most (90 per cent) of them were born into wealthy, educated families and spent their early childhood in Eastern Europe.[1] When war broke out, the oldest joined the Resistance at the age of fourteen or fifteen (8 per cent). One in three was sent to the death camps and 59 per cent were hidden.

The children who survived the camps have lived a life of constant depression. The experience of children who were hidden was similar. They were less damaged by the realities of war, but their personalities developed around a taboo about saying who they were: 'If you tell anyone who you are, you will die and the people who love you will die because of you.' After having experienced real horrors, many of those who survived the camps then found that there was a cultural taboo on bearing witness: 'What happened to you is horrifying and disgusting, so don't talk about it. You have to turn over a new leaf.' In both cases, the survivors grew up to be adults who continued to respond to the image inscribed in their memories: 'You are dangerous and disgusting.' For them, the end of the war was just the beginning of a new way of being unhappy.

Relatively few of the older children who joined the Resistance suffered from chronic depression. The self-image contained in their memories was a victorious image. Despite all that they had suffered, they were proud, and their feeling of pride was exhilarating, even though they were unhappy.

No matter when or in what circumstances they were traumatized, almost all of them displayed two features that are characteristic of damaged survivors: guilt and hypermemory. Curiously enough, their feeling of guilt socialized them. Because they were hypersensitive to all that was wrong with the world, the only way they could assuage their painful feelings was to fling themselves into the fight for a better society. So they read books, met people, became angry, laughed and loved, and thus acquired several resilience factors. Those children who grew up in an environment that prevented them from becoming involved in this way found it difficult to become resilient.

The hypermemory of the traumatized is either a sequel to what happened to them or a personal strength, depending on how their family or the social context allows them to use it. When their environment prevents them from reworking their memories, they remain prisoners of the past. The images that were imprinted on their brains by the extreme emotions triggered by the traumatic event explain the revivis-cence of the terrifying figures that they think about during the day and which come back to them in the form of nightmares when they are asleep. When, however, their families, neighbours and culture give them the opportunity to express themselves, their hypermemory adds to the accuracy of the representa-tions of the ideas, artistic productions and philisoph-ical commitments which, by giving a meaning to their damaged lives, supply them with valuable resilience factors. When we move further away from the hyper-memory of the trauma, they have few points of refer-ence because subjects who become fascinated by their aggressors do not have the mental agility of a securely attached child. Anyone who has been traumatized can either submit to his history or break free from it by using it. He has to choose between being forced to repeat it and escaping it.

Pain and Reconstruction: What Are We Transmitting?[2]

When we draw up a balance for the last fifty years, we find that most Holocaust survivors did, despite everything, have families and become part of society once more. Their inner worlds are sometimes painful and they have a distinct existential style. The truly surprising thing is that their private difficulties have not prevented them from having very successful lives. Perhaps the obligation to escape the horror had the opposite effect of making them exceptionally brave. Having had to fight so as not to go under helped them to succeed in life because they could dissociate their success from what was still a painful inner world.

Children who do very well at school probably use similar defences.[3] An anxious child feels ill at ease as soon as he takes his nose out of his book. School is the only thing that gives an abused child some dignity. A child who has been abandoned feels loved only when she is at school. The only way the child of immigrant parents can make something of their sufferings is by becoming a social success. All these examples of morbid courage explain why social success can go hand in hand with personal difficulties. For the subject's neurotic defences, their paradoxical success stories are a secondary gain. Many children who are anxious or fearful in a social context feel good about themselves only within the structured framework of a school or in an institutional environment. This form of adaptation may lead to success at school or in society, but it cannot be called resilience. Before we can speak of 'resilience', the subject must begin to rework his idea of his wound in emotional terms. Now, the paradoxical success stories that exploit a psychotrauma by adapting to it do not rework any representations. This is not resilience and, what is more, this type of defence allows the psychotrauma to re-emerge at a later date; the subject thought it had been forgotten, but it had simply been avoided or buried. It is therefore possible to come back to life after the psychic death caused by a psychotrauma, provided that the subjective preconditions are articulated within a cultural environment that can act as a resilience tutor. When that is the case, a resilient parent can become a strange parent who both fascinates and worries the child who has to grow up in contact with him.

We now have a linguistic-ethological method that allows us to observe how the inner world of such parents can tutor the development of the children who become attached to them. This is not a matter of thought-transmission, but the parents' psyches do influence their development in a particular way.

Mary Main was the first to outline this argument.[4] The time of the soul is not the time of the world, but the way in which we talk about it does transpose part of the soul and bring it into the world.[5] That is why Main began by analysing the narrative structure of pregnant women. Twelve months later, she observed how the women's children established emotional exchanges with them. After a further eighteen months, she looked at how the children became attached to their fathers. The findings are clear: the mother's inner world and the way she talks allow us to predict how her child will learn to love. But the mere presence of the father can modify that style.

In schematic terms, there appear to be four narrative styles that bring parts of the soul into the world of things:

- A 'secure-autonomous' discourse in which the semantic memory is congruent with the episodic memory, and in which the words describe memories of adequate images: 'I really liked it when my mother asked me to pack a suitcase to take on holiday.'
- A 'dismissive' discourse which keeps the two

forms of memory apart. Verbal presentations may be divorced from representations of images: 'My mother was good to me . . . She locked me in my room while she went on holiday.'

- A 'preoccupied' discourse that is vigilant and fascinated by some past ordeal: 'I keep thinking about what happened to me. I can still see myself in the cupboard. I still see images of my mother going away on holiday. I try to understand.'
- A 'confused' or dazed discourse expressed in disorganized words that bring fragments of a confused soul into the real world: 'My mother went away and left me in the cupboard. Went on holiday without me.'

A year later, the children were observed in the standardized situation that allows us to describe how they love. To put it in schematic terms, they displayed four emotional styles:[6]

- Serene attachment in children whose mothers' discourse was secure twelve months earlier, or before they were born;
- Avoidant attachment in the children of mothers with a dismissive narrative style;
- Ambivalent attachment in children whose mothers were preoccupied when they talked;

- Confused attachment in children whose mothers were disordered.

It is therefore not the content of the mother's inner world that is passed on to her child. Part of the mother's soul is put into words. It creates the child's sensorial environment and teaches it a style of loving. These scenarios for verbal behaviour become routine at the developmental stage where the child has a biological hypermemory, but the way a mother speaks tutors her child's emotional learning processes.

Physical Intimacy and Mental Transmission

The process of transposing part of the mental world and imprinting it on others has long been observed in animals. When a young female macaque is kept in isolation, the emotional deprivation she suffers will have a major impact on the way she develops. When she reaches puberty, her hormones will prime her for sex, but her deprived development has not allowed her to learn the ritual interaction that facilitates sexual encounters. The presence of male macaques arouses her and she approaches them but, because she is frightened by her own inability to interact with them, she bites them or runs away from them. She therefore has to be caught and given artificial insemination. A few months later, her newborn baby cannot detach itself from its mother. It follows her everywhere, never takes its eyes off her and watches her every move. Because it is fascinated by its inadequate mother, it cannot learn to play and therefore be socialized into the world of the other little macaques. When it reaches puberty and is primed for sex by its hormones, it approaches the females it is attracted to and bites them or runs away – just as its mother did long before it was born! Direct observation of this pathology will never allow us to understand that the origins of the young monkey's disorder lie in the emotional deprivation its mother experienced when she was little. Even with animals, we have to undertake longitudinal studies if we wish to solve the problem of intergenerational transmission.

After a few years of study, we succeeded in demonstrating that the mental worlds of dog owners can shape the way their pets behave.[7] A young couple bought an elegant Dalmatian and then adopted the whiskery stray they called 'Fleas'. The pedigree Dalmatian was top dog until the couple divorced. When the dogs were in the home of the woman, who liked the elegant Dalmatian better, Fleas was quite happy to be the underdog. He let the favourite eat first, slept in a corner and kept out of the Dalmatian's way. But when they were with the man, who liked Fleas better, the relationship was inverted. Here, it was the Dalmatian who was the underdog. He put his tail between his legs, lost his appetite, jumped at the slightest noise, suffered urinary incontinence and kept out of the way of Fleas. Thanks to the physical proximity, an inner representation from the human world can be transmitted without a word being said. It is mediated by the biology of interactions. It has an emotional impact on the dog's world and can either let it flourish or hold it back.

At about this time, family researchers noted that some emotions were, for better or worse, passed down from generation to generation in the form of 'debts' or 'conflicts of loyalty'.[8] The living world appeared to be organized around a chain of forces which, having been extracted from one mental world, could modify other mental worlds. 'It took psychoanalysts quite a long time to integrate this concept [of transgenerational transmission] into their models, but it is now integral to them.'[9]

No one now denies that the parents' state of mind, the history that made them cheerful or sad and that gives a private meaning to every object and every event, also structures their children's self-images. Intersubjectivity is not thought-transmission, and yet one person's inner representations can modify the way others feel about themselves. The medium for the transmission is attachment: gestures, some of them tiny, facial expressions and narratives act as transmitters and give the emotions their power.[10]

This has been confirmed by many experiments,[11] and we can now understand how a wound or resilience can be handed down from one generation to the next.

Mental worlds are propagated by the ritual interaction that takes place between a mother and her child. In fact, all attachment figures have this power. Fathers, brothers and sisters, friends and anyone who is loved can modify, heighten or destroy a basic emotional style, depending on how the various emotional styles are combined. When a father talks about his past relationship with his own parents, he is actually describing how he learned to love. We can therefore predict how he will bring up his children in the future. This sensorial bubble of gestures, smiles and verbal music wraps the child in an envelope of signifiers. That is how the perceptible part of the father's story is materialized and imprinted on the child's memory.

Transmitting Ways of Loving

With this type of transmission, it is difficult to say that a single cause has a single effect, as the impression transmitted to the child by a maternal wound may be modified by the father's history, then by the emotional reactions of the child's friends and family and, finally, by the stories the culture tells about the wound. Each of these sources brings pressure to bear and leaves a memory imprint whose strength depends upon the attachment style and the emotional distance involved. If the woman in the baker's tells me she does not love me, I might be upset for a few seconds, but if my wife said the same thing there would be serious consequences.

This explains why not all attachments are transmitted in the same way. If we observe how the bond is negotiated in a population of mothers with a 'preoccupied' narrative style, we immediately see that they are constantly on the alert and are worried about their past. But we also find that not all the children are affected and that a far from negligible number of them succeed in learning a serene attachment, even though they are all in contact with over-burdened and anxious mothers.[12]

Two types of bond are easily passed on: the secure attachment that allows the child to enjoy growing up, and the disordered attachment in which all information provokes distress. Other attachments are passed on less easily because the child's environment also includes a father, a big sister, a school friend, a priest or a sports monitor who allows the child to establish other bonds. The child can cling to them and thus avoid what would otherwise be an inevitable transmission. This task, which is performed almost unconsciously, is easy in a serene environment but it becomes painful if the family is in distress. A resilient evolution is, however, still possible because the child can acquire other attachments.[13] It should also be recalled that the affection the mother displays towards her child is always modified by her bond with her husband. Even day-to-day care routines are modified by those around the mother. According to Winnicott, looking after a mother in ways that recognize the essential nature of her task is all it takes to show her that she has an aptitude for holding.[14] Winnicott's words remind me of a lady who had been seriously abused by her father. She explained to me that at the precise moment when she was giving birth to her little boy, she suffered a violent attack of anxiety. 'I saw my father between my legs,' she said. This example illustrates the extent to which we respond to something we can perceive in the present tense (the child that is being born) and relate it to a self-image that has been imprinted in our memory (an abusive childhood). The lady went on: 'When I am alone with my son, I keep thinking about my father, and I abuse my child to stop myself doing so. But if my husband is there, that is enough to make me feel that I am his wife, and I no longer feel the same way about the baby.'

We can deduce from this observation that cultures which organize family systems in which children have multiple attachments afford them greater emotional protection and, should something go wrong, increase the possibility of resilience. Provided that we do not confuse multiple attachments that provide a security that is both routine and stimulating with groups of drones who come and go and make all attachments impossible. When everything is in a state of constant change, the environment does not give the child enough time to imprint its memory with a relational style which, because it is repeated, becomes a personality trait. An unstable system increases the probability that insecure attachments will develop. This is another way of saying that a child must be brought up by a group of adults who are differentiated in terms of their age and roles, but united in terms of their affections and projects.

This brings us to the schema developed by British psychoanalysts.[15] If a child is surrounded by emotional chaos, a disordered attachment will probably be imprinted on its learning processes, but if, on the contrary, a child grows up in an emotional prison, the psychotrauma suffered by its mother or attachment figure will be transmitted directly to the child.

Madame Lou had a terrifying childhood. Both her parents were alcoholics who fought constantly and beat their children every day – literally. Madame Lou kept on saying 'I hate men' because she thought men were to blame for all her problems. She did what it takes to have a baby. She had just enough sex to have the baby she believed would bring her every happiness. As soon as she became pregnant, she dismissed the 'sperm donor', who could scarcely be called a 'father' and found herself alone with the baby in which she had invested all her hopes, just as she had hoped she would be. As soon as the baby was delivered, the mother panicked and screamed at the nursing staff: 'Quick, do something! You can see she wants to die.' The baby was beautiful and in good health, and was simply doing what a baby should be doing: breathing, suckling and sleeping. The mother was projecting her own fascination with death on to her baby and then panicked when she saw what she had projected. Their first year together was a period of passionate love, with the mother organizing her life around her baby. She alternated between moments of happiness and periods of terrible anxiety about death whenever the baby had a slight cold or a digestive spasm. The little girl was just over three when her mother phoned the psychologist in tears because the child had struck her and she did not know what to do. When the girl was ten, she said: 'I've got a pain in my tummy, and I hope it's serious.' She was twelve when she declared: 'I would like to die together with my mother, but I would like a man to kill us.' When she reached adolescence, Madame Lou's sister, who had also been abused but who had developed a form of resilience, was, fortunately, able to put some distance between the tragic partners. The emotional prison constructed by a distressed mother who saw her baby as her only hope of life, had, in practice, allowed the mother to transmit the content of her thoughts. In her attempt to overcome her own emotional distress, the mother had invested too many hopes in her baby and had imagined that they would be perfectly happy together. The mother's representation had triggered in her baby 'a hypnotic relationship . . . a real imprinting . . . that launched the psychological construction of a dual relationship'.[16] But this exclusive imprinting meant that she experienced the slightest separation as a kind of abandonment and was reduced to total despair. The mother kept saying: 'I don't want her to talk to other people, because that would take her away from me . . . I don't want her to have friends, I don't want her to love anyone but me . . . I don't want her to go to school.' A securely attached mother would have been delighted and relieved to see her daughter growing up and escaping from her apron strings. Madame Lou felt intensely happy when she held her daughter tight. But that ecstasy almost immediately awakened her anxiety about being abandoned because the girl wanted to talk to other people and go to school. This way of loving allowed her to transmit her thoughts because the little prisoner could not encounter a different style of attachment that might have allowed her to escape from her mother's terrifying love. The imprinting was passed from soul to soul because mother and daughter were so close that there was no possibility of escape.

We can use words to distance ourselves in emotional terms and to see things from the outside, provided that we can talk to someone in order to facilitate our withdrawal. The way in which we speak creates a sensorial bubble, an envelope of signifiers that surrounds the child; the signifiers seep into the child through the channels of communication that have been established between the bonded partners. It is unusual for this environment to be exclusive. In most cases, the mother and child love each other, and that prevents the situation from becoming one of emotional capture. The existence of a constellation of attachments protects the child. Conversely, when the situation does become one of emotional capture, confused mothers will transmit a confused attachment in 90 per cent of cases. Secure mothers transmit a secure attachment in only 75 per cent of cases, either because the father leaves a less favourable imprint or because a sister or some other member of the family group becomes involved in establishing a more difficult bond. Only 50 per cent of avoidant or ambivalent mothers, on the other hand, pass on their relational difficulties because their children feel ill at ease with them and try to look to others for developmental support. Emotional transmission is a tendency that can be modified if the environment supplies the child with an envelope of alternative attachments. The child can then escape from its parent's unhappiness.

How to Pass On a Trauma

Lucie was five when her parents, who were both journalists, first employed Irène, who had just come back from Auschwitz. The young woman was delighted and left her own two children with the foster families who had hidden them during the war. They were very happy there and Irène felt ashamed when she turned up looking like a ghost. In the journalists' home, everyone was cheerful all the time because no one was obsessed with the horrors of the past. Irène felt that she would be able to come back to life there, but when she went back to her family home everyone knew that she had lost her husband and two of her children. The mere presence of those familiar eye-witnesses reminded her of the horrors she wanted to run away from. Irène loved life and wanted to leave the past behind. The silent presence of those members of her family who had survived prevented her from doing so, but in the journalists' home, all the talk was of the future. For a few years, everything was perfect and she was happy again, now that the nightmare was over. Such euphoria would have been shocking in her birth family, where everyone was in mourning, but both the journalists smiled and talked about Irène's strength of character. She was vaguely ashamed of feeling so happy, but avoided looking back at her past. Part of her was enjoying her day-to-day life. She joined in the party by dreaming up lovely surprises for the children of the neighbourhood, trips to the theatre and impromptu parties, and by singing sweet Yiddish songs to get Lucie to sleep at night. Irène was happy, and she had a talent for being happy.

Irène's dark side slowly began to take over and the shadow of the past began to return each evening. Her happiness was beginning to feel less secure. Little Lucie adored Irène and the ease with which she could turn the slightest little thing into poetry. One night, the child asked her to translate a song because it was sweet, so beautiful and so sad: '*Es brennt, brideler, es brennt . . .*' 'Why's it burning?' asked Lucie. Irène was flooded with anxiety. 'Flooded' is the right word. This was not what we usually call a sudden anxiety attack. This was a flood of images and emotions that suddenly overwhelmed her. The Irène who sang, who was always laughing and who talked so much, had locked away part of her past and her personality. It was as though it had been locked away in a safe – or a coffin. Her origins lay in death: her husband, two of her children and many of her friends and neighbours were all dead. Her culture was dead and her country of origin was dead. How could someone who loved life live with all that? We avoid survivors and people who remind us of the dead. Only a tiny part of them is still alive. You laugh and talk and sing when you have the good fortune to be a governess in such a nice family and when a child pays you the compliment of loving you.

Irène had to answer Lucie's question. As she was putting her to bed, she told her how, one day, the really nice neighbour who used to come around every night to eat creamed herrings and to have a glass of vodka turned up with thirty men she did not know, smashed up the house and kicked her father to death. She told her how her children, who were so sweet, so clean and so well brought up, both disappeared. The last time she saw them they were filthy and emaciated. She told her about the mindless violence of the police, about her feeling of imminent death, about how their neighbours denounced her and her family, and about how the passers-by humiliated them.

That same evening Lucie suffered the first symptoms of a psychotrauma triggered by a horror that she had not experienced but which her beloved Irène had passed on. It had been transmitted from Irène's soul to Lucie's.

Splitting mechanisms had allowed Irène to suffer less from the horrors of the past. Part of her personality flourished in the real post-war world, but she kept another part – the dark part – at a distance in order to stop the pain returning. Sometimes the young woman even invented an imaginary past that allowed her to deny the terrifying reality of what had happened. When the terrible memories returned in her moments of solitude, Irène protected herself by imagining that she had sent the two sons she had lost to buy some milk just before the militiamen arrived, and that she had saved their lives. She enjoyed that illusion. Sometimes she invented a different scenario in which she modified her memory of her father's murder. The kind neighbour did not smash up the house and kick her father to death. He intervened and stopped the lynch mob by explaining that this hard-working family had not done anything wrong. The mob immediately calmed down and left. Modifying this representation of her story allowed Irène to be happier in the here and now, but it did not help her to face up to her unhappy past. As soon as she allowed her vigilance to lapse, as soon as she stopped being cheerful and stopped doing all the inventive, generous and poetic things that the family liked so much, traces of the past emerged once more. They had been contained by her suppression of all feelings and emotions, but they had not been reshaped by the work of resilience.

That is why, when Lucie and her governess, who had such emotional trust in each other, were getting ready for bed that night, those terrible words had rung out in the darkness of the bedroom just as the child was going to sleep. The psychotrauma was transmitted directly from Irène's soul to Lucie's. From that night onwards, Lucie had nightmares for forty years. She was convinced that the neighbours were going to break in and smash up the house. But she is now doing resilience work that Irène was unable to do. The grown-up Lucie is now coming to terms with Irène's past and doing research on the Holocaust. She is politically active, which is how she met her husband. It is Lucie who is reworking the emotions caused by the horrors of the past and giving a meaning to the wound that was passed on by Irène's stories.

The governess had adapted to intense but contradictory impulses: an overwhelming desire to be happy, and the immense suffering caused by the fact that so many of her family had been killed. Without meaning to, the journalist couple had made the splitting process worse by applauding the living half of her personality and discouraging her from thinking about the past. In psychic terms, Irène was surviving in pleasant surroundings. She was living in a household where no one had suffered because of the war, whereas the few members of her family to have survived were living alongside their dead. The dead would have felt abandoned if they had stopped talking about them, and would have felt betrayed if they had allowed themselves to be happy when they were dead. The cheerful

Irène was faced with a stark choice: she could either live with the survivors, and in the company of the dead, or she could use splitting mechanisms so as to snatch a little happiness and a desperate hope as she awaited death. Her resilience allowed the representation of her unhappiness to undergo a gradual metamorphosis, but the splitting that preserved her immediate happiness later allowed the ghosts to return.

This does not mean that talking about death protects our loved ones. It was at this time that the French Communist Party began to describe itself as 'the party of those who were shot'. Over 10,000 Communists were either executed after summary trials or murdered in prisons and death camps. I knew survivors who came back full of rage, and who are still outraged by what they had seen and suffered. They talked, screamed, remembered, commemorated, published, organized meetings and papered the walls with horrific photographs. All their children required psychiatric treatment. Once they came home, these survivors lived in such close emotional proximity to their families that they passed on their traumas intact. The real, for its part, is always ambivalent. There is always a reassuring gesture in the midst of the greatest terror, a smile in the greatest horror and a patch of the sky is always blue, even in Auschwitz. The children of the deported Communists were given a representation of pure, unadulterated horror, and it was made worse by their parents' desire to convince others. They were forced to wallow in their atrocity stories day by day. For their parents, this was a case of legitimate self-defence. The Communist Party used these images as a political argument, and their children grew up in a world where abomination was always imminent. They did not dare go into their bedrooms at night because they imagined that there were piles of corpses on their beds. They expected the class enemy to break in and kill them. Many of them suffered panic attacks.

There were more secrets than we thought, but because they were secrets, no one talked about them much and we concluded there were not many of them. Ever since the concept of resilience was developed in Europe, in the Americas and in the Middle East, I have received an astonishing number of friendly anonymous letters: 'My Dear Colleague, you will understand why I have not signed this letter if I tell you that I was born in 1943. My father, who was a German soldier, died in the debacle of 1944. My mother had to put me in an orphanage. The only way for me to make my way in life and to get an education was to keep quiet and tell no one about my background. If I'd talked about it, I'd have been rejected. Sixty years later, my profession is the same as yours. I am a psychiatrist, but I still have to keep quiet about my childhood.'[17]

It is said that 200,000 children in France were born as a result of relationships between German soldiers and French civilians. No crimes were committed. On the contrary, the personalities of these young parents were strong enough to resist the environmental pressures and stigmatization: 'A Boche is a brute . . . A Frenchwoman is a slut.' These young people were not subjected to the scornful stereotypes of the day that allowed the structuring of groups that needed to hate before they could go to war. They fell in love with individuals and not prejudices. Couples who are in love escape social, religious and ideological pressures. In the context of a war, this kind of love affair means 'treason', but in peacetime it means 'tolerance'. The act of love is the same in all cultures but, depending on the social context, it can also be an act of treachery or a fine romance.

Those Frenchwomen who were seduced by Nazism were in a very different position. Many of them were married and belonged to social groups which collaborated with the enemy. It is improbable that many children were born of that complicity.

Some high-ranking Nazis were given refuge and protection in Syria after the war. Their children, who are fully integrated there, are proud of their heroic SS fathers. They have not had to keep quiet about their origins and loudly chant Hitlerite slogans. What is passed on to children whose parents have suffered a trauma depends as much on the way the wounded talk about their wounds as on how their cultures turn them into myths.

Hélène was proud of having defended herself by having her father sent to prison. He had raped her for years and had involved her in sadistic sex games. Having defended herself – quite legitimately – in court, she then published a book in which she insisted that incest occurs in the real world; at the time it was thought that it existed only in fantasies. And then she met a kind man and had a little boy with him. Hélène had succeeded in modifying her culture which, thanks to her, had discovered a sexual violence whose existence it used to deny, but she did not have enough time to teach passers-by respect. People would stop her in the street and ask her, in the presence of her child: 'Is that your father's boy or your husband's?' Part of his mother's trauma had been passed on to the boy, and it was now modified by the shamelessness of a few passers-by. The day after he heard them say this, the little boy began to suffer from enuresis and to exhibit symptoms of anxiety.

Interpreting What Has Been Passed On

The role the children of traumatized parents play in passing on the psychotrauma is not a passive one, as they have acquired a preferential perception of the world. They interpret it and react to it with their own emotional style. Peter had always known that his father survived Auschwitz but, because he kept quiet about it or talked about it only in vague terms, the boy stopped himself from asking certain questions:

FATHER: I didn't want to tell him about the horrors
   I'd been through. I wanted to protect him.
SON: I used to avoid talking about the subjects he
   wanted to avoid.

The father wanted to protect his son, and the son wanted to obey his father's non-verbal command. Order reigned, but so did the suffering. It was like some insidious disease that slowed down their exchanges because they wanted so much to remain in control. Both men were in fact trapped in an emotional misunderstanding and the way in which each of them tried to protect the other was damaging their relationship.

   In some cases, the damaged father had become so weak that the child felt that, when he came back, he cast a chill over their day-to-day life. The child felt ill at ease inside this envelope of weighty signifiers. Until the ghost returned, he was happy with his mother but, when he was overwhelmed by unhappiness, he interpreted his discomfort in aggressive terms: 'The reason why dad came back from the camps is that he made a deal with the Nazis. If he had been brave and honest, he'd be dead.'

This damaged self-image is a product of the convergence of several narratives. The subjective narrative the child repeats inside his head constitutes his narrative identity, but it is also shaped by the pressures brought to bear by the narratives he hears around him. Some families turned their reunion into a thing of joy, whilst others kept the wound open. And the cultural context usually gives rise to a feeling of shame rather than pride. 'When we attempt to help people to become mentally resilient, we therefore rely upon those processes that help to preserve psychic envelopes . . . exchanges between the individual and the environment . . . exchanges within the family, its system of values and beliefs.'[18] Our self-image feeds on the scraps of reality that our families and our culture put at our disposal.

Claire's father was five (in 1942) when he was taken into care by Entraide temporaire, a clandestine organization that saved some 500 Jewish children.[19] Claire, who was born in 1962, never called her parents 'mum' and 'dad', probably because they never referred to themselves in those terms. 'My childhood was organized around the sore my father had developed as a child. I grew up with the part of him that had died . . . He was incapable of calling my mother "mum", and used to say: "Go and ask Rose." When he wrote to us, he signed his letters with his first name and never with "dad".

'"Hello, dad?"

'"Who's speaking?"'[20]

Someone who is not inscribed in a line of descent does not feel that they can become a father in their turn, and therefore sees no reason why anyone should call them 'dad'. The way in which we capture a self-image impregnates our memory, and that memory feeds on the scraps of reality that are provided by those around us.

Bracinho knew he was a gypsy, but he did not know what it meant to be a gypsy. His parents had settled in the Lisbon area and he was born there. His father, who was a mason, was killed in an accident at work when the boy was two. His mother vanished two years later and handed her little boy over to a social worker. He heard people around him saying: 'They're dirty . . . they're uncouth . . . they steal our chickens and kill our children in human sacrifices.' Bracinho said to himself that he came from a human group that was very ugly and very terrifying. The persecution did not make him angry but he knew it was unfair because, not knowing any other gypsies, he felt vaguely ashamed about coming from a group like that. He planned to stop being a gypsy but felt none of the shame that is usually felt by those who abandon their original group in order to become part of a different culture. There was no room in his inner world for the psychical court that condemns traitors. In his daydreams, he imagined that, on the contrary, a sort of jury would allow him to prove himself innocent. When a culture condemns us to be driven out of humanity for a crime we did not know we had committed, some court of appeal has to find us innocent. That is why so many victims feel the strange need to bear witness in public in order to rehabilitate themselves.

Bracinho was on trial before a court made up of normal Portuguese people. But the boy pleaded his case so well that he proved he was not a bandit, that he was not uncouth and that he had never stolen any chickens. So his judges admitted their mistake and accepted the young gypsy. But was he a gypsy? Bracinho felt guilty, not because he had betrayed his family and friends – he had none – but because he came from a culture he knew nothing about and because it prevented him from being like everyone else. He often imagined himself in front of a court and was surprised at how glad he felt when he was found innocent. 'I know I'm a gypsy,' he would say to himself, 'but I don't know what a gypsy is. I'm something I know nothing about.'

One morning, he was hanging about on the Praça do Comércio on the banks of the Tagus, hoping to find someone to play with, and was drawn to a little group of men playing guitars. The musicians were dark skinned, had white teeth, wore strange clothes, and had drawn a small crowd. Their songs were a revelation to Bracinho. For the first time in his life, he saw that there was something beautiful about being a gypsy. The audience seemed to share his happiness. So it was possible to be a gypsy and to be accepted by society! A tall, rather heavily built man wearing a cap and leather trousers came up to the boy: 'Vulgar music, always the same.' Bracinho promised himself he would hit the man when he was big enough, and then went back to the music he was enjoying so much. But two things astonished him. He remembered the cap and the leather trousers so that he would be able to recognize his aggressor and give him a good hiding, and he had carefully watched the musicians who had, for the first time, made him happy because he belonged.

A snatch of music and a fragmentary image had supplied some raw material for a self-image. Bracinho felt better because his everyday culture had given him two or three scraps of information that he could use to begin to construct the beginnings of a self-image. He realized that there were others like him. Bracinho suddenly felt an urge to go in search of his origins in order to preserve this new feeling of well-being, of quiet strength and – how shall I put it – of having grown bigger. Tiny scraps of signifiers – music, dark skin – acted as an invitation to explore the archaeology of knowledge, the art of the archives, old photos, objects from elsewhere and encounters to come. As he began to work on these signifiers, his feeling of self was preparing to undergo a metamorphosis that would help him make the transition from a vague feeling of shame to a well-documented sense of pride.

When the revelation of what has not been said takes place within a relationship of emotional capture, the psychotrauma is passed on very easily, as we saw in the case of little Lucie's excessive attachment to her governess Irène. When, on the other hand, a child discovers its origins ('I don't know what it means to be a gypsy') thanks to cultural scraps of images, music, stories or documents, he or she experiences the same pleasure as an archaeologist.

A Silent Din

A lot of trauma victims find it easier to write about their suffering than to talk about it with a close friend or relative, because writing allows them to remain in control of their feelings. Even in a public broadcast, where there is a great emotional distance between the speaker and his or her invisible listeners, the emotion is not as strong as it would be in a face-to-face discussion with a loved one, where it might distort or even block communications.

When we feel ashamed, we leave certain things unsaid or find it difficult to talk about them. We allude to them, talk about them in roundabout ways and stumble over our words, which is why there are so many misunderstandings. In a noisy context, any silence attracts attention, just as we become vigilant when a background noise stops. 'Why the sudden calm? What's happening?' A sudden silence on the part of a man who is a good speaker makes anyone who is attached to him feel that there is something strange and enigmatic about him: 'In the same way that the negative of a photo indicates what is there without revealing it.'[21] Speech transmits what it reveals, and that can traumatize a child who is too attached. When silence is part of the narrative and of the meeting of mental worlds, it casts a worrying shadow on what is being discovered or projected. It is astounding to hear the children of traumatized parents saying that they saw the trauma in their nightmares, even when their parents thought they had kept it hidden.

'When the genocide began on 7 April 1994, we were on our Easter holidays . . . Our little brothers were staying with relatives. We thought we would all see each other again in a fortnight, but we never did. They didn't survive.'[22] This often happens in the genocides and military coups that modern wars inflict upon children and civilians. When someone disappears, we initially hope that we will see the survivors come back. Gradually, we have to accept that they are not coming back and that they have no graves. We were not there when the others were killing them. We could not help them. Perhaps we were even happy while they were dying. We are filled with shame. They killed them and left their bodies (it hurts to add 'to rot where they lay'). We weren't up to the task.

We can overcome this feeling of shame by making sure that all the dead get a decent burial. When those close to us die like this, we learn to care about the dignity of the dead. 'Whenever I see a film about Rwanda, I look to see if my brothers are among the survivors. They are still alive inside my head and everything reminds me of them. I also look for them when I see photos of piles of corpses. It's as though they had died today.' This silent preoccupation with death finds expression in bodily indices to which children are extremely sensitive: the frozen silence of a mother as she waits for her disappeared brother to appear on the TV screen, the tiny twitch of the mouth when a kindly neighbour congratulates her on having escaped the genocide. These silent signifiers cast a shadow over what is being said and give children the feeling that something disturbingly enigmatic is going on: 'What is happening back there to make my mother go quiet when anyone talks about Rwanda?' There is something unclear about the way they died. Perhaps an evil spell was put on them. Perhaps they were murdered. Above all, ask no questions. The child goes to sleep with the disquiet that has been transmitted by her mother's shame. At night, she has bad dreams in which she sees her mother's body rotting where it lies, as the passers-by laugh until their sides ache. In her inner world, the child is acting out the shame that is torturing her mother.

VI

Sombre Songs

The Flesh of Ghosts

'I'm frightened of the dark,' said the child. 'When it's dark, the dead rise from their graves.' Perhaps he had imagined it – the darkness had taken on the tear-stained faces and forgotten smiles of people he didn't know. 'I didn't know anything about them, except that they were dead.' A child whose nightmares feed on his family's shame feels different and disturbing. How can you face your parents when you are haunted by their shame?

He had been told quite clearly not to talk to the soldiers. He remembered the day when, as he was playing on the embankment, his ball rolled under a bench where two soldiers were chatting. They gave it back to him with a few kind words he could not understand. A few days later, his parents disappeared after having been arrested by the militia. They were deported and died in the camps. For years, the boy told himself over and over again that he must have said something when the soldiers gave him his ball back. Without meaning to, he had obviously given them a few clues, and that had led to his parents' arrest. He had not been able to keep the secret and they died as a result. That is why, for decades, he admired people who could keep quiet. Silence made him feel safe. But his shame at having let slip a few words and his guilt at having brought about the death of his parents had taught him to behave strangely: he could only talk about trivial things because all intimacy felt to him like a disturbing intrusion.

Being ashamed does not transmit the same feeling as 'bearing shame'.[1] Bracinho the gypsy was ashamed of what he was. He did not know what he was, but his culture suggested to him that it was something to be ashamed of. Once he was able to identify a constructive model, a resilience process allowed him to make the transition from being ashamed to being proud. This working-through process is very different from 'bearing shame', which means suffering because we have attachments. This makes the resilience process even more costly: 'Before I can stop being ashamed of something I can't put a name to, I have to make reparation for my parents' discomfort.' A few glimpses of gypsy culture were enough to make Bracinho stop feeling ashamed, but a boy who 'brings shame' knows nothing about the problem he has to confront and often feels that he is being attacked by the parent he loves: 'I don't know why I feel ill at ease when I'm with my father and in despair when he isn't there.' The child was living with a father who had a hole in him. Sometimes he was pleasant but he was often sombre. This was the father he had had to grow up with. He had picked up something of this ashamed behaviour, and as a result he alternated between feeling numb and feeling an emotional warmth. He had acquired an ambivalent attachment, whereas his wounded and ashamed parent was convinced that he was protecting him by saying nothing. But because he was a slave to happiness, his father did not realize that he had passed on to his son the disturbing sensation of being simultaneously happy and anxious. 'All success makes me feel guilty. I feel less ill at ease when failure drives me to despair,' as the bringer of shame might put it.

The power of ghosts is neither magical nor ectoplasmic. On the contrary, their power comes from a physical perception of something strange, of a gesture, an intonation or a silence that allows the child to see them appearing on the body of a loved one. Ghosts have no life of their own. They need the body of someone who has been hurt before they can summon up death or the suffering and shame that will feed off the child's mind. An event from the past casts a shadow on the wounded body, and the ghosts transmit it from one soul to another.

'I would like my children to keep well clear of the path I have to take,' the father thought to himself when he came back from Auschwitz. 'I would like them to travel to more peaceful places and to have a childhood in which they know no fear.'

His son says nothing but quietly thinks to himself: 'My father thinks that this hidden side to him is something worthy of hatred. I've known for a long time that something has to remain buried. Without saying a word, my father very definitely gave me to understand that I must not look in that direction,' he adds in his internal monologue.[2]

Gloomy Parent, Prickly Child

This forbidden dialogue, which is perceived on the bodies of the interlocutors and which derives from their internal languages, illustrates the degree to which an emotional misunderstanding can be transmitted from one soul to another when there is an attachment.

The young people who survived the camps married extremely young. At the time, having a husband or a wife was a major protective factor. Men could not survive without wives when they had to walk to work and then put in a ten-hour day. Women could not survive without husbands in a technological context in which human bodies were the main tools of social production. For a man who was impotent or weak or a woman who could not have children or was not strong enough to raise a family, the future looked bleak. This was a society in which there was no social security and no old age pensions. The young survivors over-invested in marriage because it was their only hope of coming back to life. Most formed relationships in which an anxious attachment had a therapeutic effect. When they emerged from the camps, getting married allowed them to come back to life and, in some cases, to weave their resilience.

These couples' children had to grow up in close contact with parents who were still injured and who had scarcely begun the task of convalescence. The children's developmental tutors were damaged. It was not easy for them to establish stable and transparent relationships with fathers who were brave, silent and sombre, who were kind to them on a day-to-day basis, but who could also suddenly explode with unexpected violence. Their parents put a lot of energy into looking after each other because that was the contract their relationship was based on. Their children grew up in close contact with parents who were taciturn, attentive, kind and oppressively silent. They felt excluded from their parents' loving relationships.

This explains why so many of these children experienced a sort of emotional deprivation even though their parents thought they had given them so much affection. The adults organized their lives around their children, based all their choices on their children's interests, showed them a permissive kindness and avoided any mention of their own suffering so as not to pass it on to them. The children, on the other hand, felt that they were intruding on a complicit parental couple, and resented their permissiveness as a weakness or even an abandonment. They were fascinated by the worrying shadow that their wounded parents had turned into an enigma by drawing a veil over a zone they thought they should hide. 'It is the things we overhear, and which we often do not understand, the allusions, which may or may not be emphasized, the facial expressions and the gestures, which may or may not be punctuated with meaningful silences . . . that we all use to create representations of events that took place in our prehistory.'[3]

Children who are forced to be happy learn that the slightest mishap will reduce their strange fathers to despair: 'He seemed to want so much to think only happy thoughts, to perform only serene actions . . .'[4] Because this enforced happiness makes them anxious, the children of traumatized parents often acquire an ambivalent attachment: 'I love them from inside those dark places too, from inside those dreadful places.'[5] For these children, hate is not the opposite of love. Hate means an angry rebellion against a father who has been torn apart and who is undergoing repairs. He is so gloomy that his children become prickly. It is only later that they learn to be proud of their silent parents.

Hervé said: 'I hated her whenever she was cheerful because, when she was in that mood, she would abandon me.' His father had just come back from

Algeria, where the war was at its height. He talked too much, too loudly and too cheerfully in order to hide the things he could not talk about calmly. It was because he was in contact with a father who hid his sadness behind his enforced gaiety that Hervé acquired the ambivalent attachment he would later display towards his wife. He loved her dearly when she was there and felt an angry hatred for her when she went anywhere without him.

Children who have been brought up by couples bound together by this type of contract have learned to pay attention to what is not being said, are fascinated by secrets and are both worried by and interested in sudden changes of behaviour and silences: 'That's odd! Why does she freeze when she talks about children who are born outside marriage . . . That's odd! Every time anyone mentions my father's family, my mother says, "Oh dear, oh dear," suddenly remembers there is something she has to do around the house and breaks off the conversation.' These little enigmas or tiny cracks are scarcely visible to the naked eye, but they are repeated so often that they eventually provide the child with an initiation into strangeness. It is as though he was thinking: 'There is a taboo on knowledge that both frightens me and fascinates me.' The child's inner world becomes ambivalent, and his emotional style gradually becomes just as ambivalent. 'I'm not very sure about what happened to my father when he was a boy because he finds it hard to talk about it: something is mentioned, a shadow crosses his face and my mother comes to his rescue and protects him by changing the subject. Something strange must have happened to him. Perhaps something terrible. Given the childhood he had, I have no right to complain. I have to be happy so as to justify all he has done for me. I have to succeed because he has made it possible for me to succeed and because he wasn't a success. I'd be ashamed if I wasn't a success. I hold that against him.'

Initially, this obligation to be both happy and anxious seems to produce good results as the child is loyal enough to take his place in this enigmatic line of descent. But when he reaches adolescence and begins to feel that he must leave his loved ones in order to learn to love differently, reworking his emotional bonds is often a painful process. His ambivalence steers the adolescent in the direction of either a reassuring resignation or a heady passion for archaeology. 'I'm fed up with wearing myself out trying to find the happiness my father is demanding,' said one child. 'It feels good when I stop trying.' Another child thinks: 'I'm fascinated by everything that is hidden. I become anxious when I stop trying to understand.'

Identifying with a Dead Parent

The splitting of the damaged parent who tries to protect his child by passing on only the transparent part of his personality unwittingly brings about an ambivalent attachment. This emotional style appears to be much more common in populations of children whose traumatized parents have scarcely begun to weave their resilience than in the population at large, where an estimated 5 per cent of children display this style.[6] This ambivalent way of loving 'appears to be structured around unresolved parental conflicts that lead the adult to invest in the child in order to compensate for a lack of affection'.[7] The young parents who had been traumatized by the war were eager to marry quickly because they wanted to come back to life and to have children who would love them as soon as possible. They wanted to give them all the happiness they had been denied. This adaptive defence mechanism protected the parents and passed on to their children an ambivalent attachment that lasted until they reached adolescence.

We could easily jump to conclusions and say, 'So that's where resilience gets you: the parents become resilient and the children suffer the consequences.' It has to be stressed that these parents had scarcely begun the resilience process, and that they were doing so in a culture that took no notice of them. They were still at the stage where their immediate suffering forced them to come to terms with the disaster that had just occurred. They were still in shock when, to everyone's amazement, everything flared up again. They gritted their teeth and said nothing, which is what we always do immediately after we have been hurt. It is only after the event, and when hindsight, distance and time allow us to put it into words, that we can explain ourselves. If their culture also forces the wounded to remain silent, it will take them decades to recover. It takes only a few seconds to conceive a child, but it takes years for a child to grow up. The child's parents will spend those years trying to repair themselves. The child came into the world at a time when the only thing her damaged parents wanted was to be reborn, to come back to life after their psychic death. She is now surrounded by developmental tutors who have been damaged by the wounds inflicted on her parents. That is what she has to learn to live with.

Little orphans who idealize their dead parents do quite well when they find surrogate families. But they have to inscribe themselves in two lines of descent: that of the dead family they idealized, and that of their present family that rescued them, even though it is, like all families, clumsy. They dream up two family romances which fill their inner worlds and sometimes make it hard for them to form relationships, but the results are far from negligible.

A cynic might conclude that it is better to have parents who are dead than parents who are damaged. I suggest that we listen to the family therapists who find that, when one member of the group suffers a serious illness such as cancer or a bad heart attack, her family and in-laws rally around. Other problems seem to be of secondary importance and are forgotten about because there are more important things to worry about for the moment. The relatives who rally around the invalid expect him to die. They are preparing themselves for a sombre future and feel happy about it. If, by some misfortune, the patient should recover, there is no longer any point to their adaptational projects and the problems they had put aside come to the fore again. Are we to conclude that we should kill everyone who falls ill? We would do better to negotiate, care for the patient as best we can and warn families about the risks they run if they see this ordeal as their only problem.

For similar reasons, those close to us organize a shadow zone around us when we are forced to remain silent. But the exquisite pain of a wounded soul can transmit a strange sensation to a child. Perhaps that is why it is written that 'The fathers have eaten a sour grape, and the children's teeth are set on edge.'[8] The silence that saves the damaged parent gives the child a developmental tutor who tries to obey two contra-dictory impulses: 'I am attached to a father who makes me anxious . . . I forbid myself to ask him questions about the shadow that fascinates me . . . I admire him because he is an initiate and I despise him because he has a sore that disgusts me . . . I love him because he cheers me up when he is cheerful and I hate him when his sorrow overwhelms me.' That is how chil-dren speak when their damaged parents have found it impossible to get anywhere with their resilience work.

It is almost always the family or the cultural envir-onment that prevents resilience from suturing the wound. How can we tell someone that they are the child of an incestuous relationship? The family keeps quiet so as to protect the child, who then grows up in a mental fog. How could anyone tell a child who was hidden during the Second World War that, if she admitted she was Jewish or spelled out her name, she would be responsible for the death of her loved ones? If children like this become parents before they have time to get over this curse, their parents' unhappiness will still be inside their heads as they bring up their own children. But when resilience is possible because the environment has not blocked the natural tendency to come back to life, the child will be able to grow up with a parent who has been repaired.

The Withdrawal of Damaged Parents

Mothers who have been damaged will probably still be in difficulty when they have their first child. If resilience work becomes possible either because their families rally around them when disaster strikes, because they meet a partner who can be supportive, or because they find a resilience tutor (writing, involvement in artistic or social activities, psychotherapy), and especially if society provides them with sites of resilience, they will not be the same when they have their second child.

We have known since the 1970s how a 'standard mother' interacts with her new-born baby. We can predict that a young woman who had a happy upbringing will be attentive to any signal her baby sends out. She will respond to it by smiling and by talking a lot.[9] Fathers who look after their babies smile much less, do not talk so much and are more 'motor' than women.

This is not the case with mothers who were victims of incest when they were girls. Most of the time, they are left speechless by the babies they have just given birth to. They look at them in amazement without saying a word and without moving a muscle. If we talk to them later, we find that, at this crucial point in their lives, the mental fog in which they live is haunted by an almost obsessional idea: 'What will he be like in sexual terms?' In the midst of their confusion, a vague notion then emerges: 'Pray God he doesn't experience any sexual violence.' When they look at their new-born babies, they sometimes have thoughts that they immediately put out of their minds: 'Pray God he doesn't commit any acts of sexual violence.' If the baby is a girl, the mother may have a sudden flash of insight: 'She'll be raped one day' or 'I'll kill her when she reaches adolescence.'

The mother's perception of the baby's anatomical sex reminds her of her representation of her own past misfortunes, and her response takes the form of a painful confusion shot through with sudden but terrible thoughts. That is what happens when a wounded mother is left on her own, with her past engraved on her memory. Why does she have to be left alone? Any attachment figure who stands by her when she gives birth can make her feel safe at this critical moment. If she has a partner, she feels herself to be a woman and feels happy when she sees the joy she has given him by giving him a baby. A familiar face is all it takes to change a mother's mental world.

The prophets of doom are not lying when they say that an abused child will become an abusive parent or that an incest victim will become a sexual abuser. They are simply describing the situation created by a collective consciousness which, because it assumes that traumatized children are doomed to repeat the past, abandons them and thus forces them to repeat it. If, however, we change the inner world of the mother, we change the sensorial environment in which she wraps her baby, and if we help her to chase away her ghosts, she can provide her baby with a secure environment.[10]

It tends, however, to be the opposite that happens. Mothers like this go to the opposite extreme and become over-permissive because they are under the confused impression that anyone would be better than them at bringing up a child. They feel that their husbands, an educationalist or even their other children know what to do and say in order to give her baby a happy life. There is a danger that a mother who was abused as a girl will hide behind those she loves because she has had no opportunity to discover that she herself is competent.

Fathers who have been damaged also believe that they are incapable of becoming fathers. When they meet a supportive woman, they therefore give her a great deal of power 'because she knows what she's doing'.

The children who are born of these encounters will have to grow up with some very peculiar parents. Their mothers are permissive and hide behind others, including their other children in some cases, and their fathers are incomplete and split into two. One half is quiet at home, but the other one can sometimes be a great success outside the home. Their children are astonished to find that there are two sides to their fathers and to hear them being talked about in admiring terms when they tend to be ignored at home. The ambivalence imprints itself on their memories and they thus acquire a twofold representation of these associated but contradictory images.

It is a mistake to think that children who have lived in hiding are repressed. On the contrary, they have traumatic hypermemories that are accurate, clear and always there inside them. They find it difficult to put these representations into words, or to find the words that might allow them to create a world they can share. When they become parents, they remember that they owe their lives to the fact that they were able to keep quiet when they were children. Little Armenians in Turkey, Jewish children in Europe, little Cambodians and the young Tutsis who fled the massacres in Rwanda all had to keep quiet if they wanted to stay alive.

The defence mechanism of remaining silent in order to survive gives them a particular relational style. As children, they were cheerful, active and creative and had their dreams. They grew up too quickly, and as adults they shut down and mentally freeze whenever a situation or question reminds them of what they had learned to avoid. When they were old enough to have children, the same defence mechanism was still in place. They became parents only a few years after the tragedy and, for them, self-expression was a reminder of death. The defence mechanism is engraved upon their memories because it is what saved their lives. They are like soldiers who are crossing a minefield: 'I can step there . . . I can talk about that . . . but I have to stop suddenly because my life is in danger if I say a single word.'

Destiny Is Not Development

If nothing ever changed – either inside us or around us – our destinies would be traced in advance and we would spend the rest of our lives repeating the lesson we learned at the moment when we had to keep quiet in order to survive. There would be a danger that we would pass on to our children a 'defensive exclusion'.[11] 'I keep quiet in self-defence,' a mother might say, 'and that teaches my children never to be spontaneous because they have the feeling that there is something obscure about our relationship. They never really trust me because my behavioural strategy suggests to them that there is a worrying enigma, a dead space inside me.' When children like this have to face some ordeal, they do not know how to call for help because they feel that there was something in their mothers' lives that could not be talked about. They will either sink or swim, and there will be no half-measures. The child of a parent who has not had time to weave her resilience 'remains impervious to experiences that do not fit in with the established system of representation and resists change'.[12]

Fortunately, it is impossible for nothing to change, even in a petrified society. At every stage in its development, a child changes the way it perceives the world, and every sentence it pronounces changes the world it perceives. Every social discourse founds a new institution that will tutor different developments.

Prospective methods track damaged people until they become parents and grandparents. When a disorder is observed, retrospective methods try to explain it by looking to the past and searching through life histories. The two epistemological strategies lead to very different findings.

It appears that, in certain countries, a population of 1,000 abused children will produce a population of 260 delinquent adolescents. The figure is much higher than that for the population at large.

Police officers who arrest juvenile delinquents ask them to describe their lives. The retrospective method tells us that 92 per cent of them were abused. The logical conclusion is that abuse almost always leads to delinquency. And the theory of identification with the aggressor is used to explain the phenomenon.[13] Now imagine that a youth offender worker tracks the same 1,000 children until they become adults. The prospective method reveals that 74 per cent of them develop normally and are still in emotional contact with their workers. We can therefore conclude that abuse rarely leads to delinquency.

The findings are very different, but no one is telling lies. The observers simply collect accurate data from their respective places of work and therefore see things differently. The police officer says: 'Abuse is a destiny that leads to delinquency.' The youth offender worker replies: 'If we support these children, the vast majority of them will develop normally.'

Words have the power to bring into the world concepts that allow us to observe fragments of the human condition. Once we can see them, we can discuss them, and that suddenly brings them to life in social discourses. The phenomenon of globalization existed in the real world long before anyone gave it a name, but once words brought it to life, social and cultural groups began to organize, either to resist it or to promote it.[14]

Most of the Jewish children who were hidden (during the Second World War) had no family. Their families had disappeared, either for ever or for the duration of the war. A population of 906 subjects (580 boys and 326 girls) was followed until they reached the age of eighteen.[15] It was found that how they developed depended upon which institutions looked after them or which people they met. That it is possible for them to grow up differently if they have been in different institutions or have had different relational experiences proves that resilience is a real phenomenon and that we have more control over it when it also exists in our words, our discourses, our research and our decisions.

These long-term studies overturn our prejudices. At the age of eighteen, hidden children who had been taken in by families performed better at school than children who had been in children's homes. But that form of intelligence is so malleable that they could catch up, even after they had reached the age of fifteen. Post-traumatic physical and intellectual development remains a possibility for much longer than we thought.

The children who were hidden produced a high percentage of painful biographies. Their main problems were emotional and to do with identity. It was not just that more risk factors were involved (isolation, the breaking of emotional bonds, changes of institution); they had learned to survive by suppressing part of their personality, and by erasing or blurring their self-image. How could they concentrate on becoming themselves when everyone around them was telling them that, if they opened up, it would be a kind of attempted murder? 'If you tell them who you are, you will die . . . Telling them where you come from means a death sentence for those who were kind enough to look after you . . . What little you've been given is a lot . . . The very fact that you are in our house means that you pose a threat. You'll bring us bad luck.' These children were living in an environment where they were protected and, in many cases, loved, but survival was a painful experience. They heard things that terrified them: 'The neighbour took in a little Jew like you. He talked. The Gestapo burned their farm.' Day after day, the child hears kind words that chill his soul. 'We took him in because he's all alone, because we don't know where his family is, and because he's so cute. We are risking our lives for his sake,' said the kind Hutus who saved the little Tutsi from being massacred.

Taking Risks and Gaining Acceptance

As a result of these insidious and repeated traumas, these children feel an ambivalent gratitude towards their protectors. The gift makes them anxious and the debt is so crippling that it can never be repaid. In these adverse conditions, the only children who can become resilient are those who can succeed in eroticizing danger by putting themselves to the test. The idea of playing on the edge of the grave comes to them quite naturally, and it has the effect of a divine judgement that grants them just the right to live.

Adults do not understand this absurd risk-taking, and often do not even see it, as children like this put themselves to the test in secret so that only God can see them. Given that they have been driven out of humanity and have been condemned to death simply because they exist, they cannot retake their place in the human communion unless they go through an integration rite. And given that society offers them no such rites, they find ever more cruel and dangerous ways of proving to themselves that they are stronger than death. Depending on what their environment has to offer, they might scale almost smooth walls at night and without any safety equipment, dive into the sea during storms, pick fights for no reason and without feeling any hatred for anyone, or take sexual risks without experiencing any desire.

This is why, contrary to what our prejudices tell us, many girls who were victims of incest do survive the ordeals they put themselves through after their terrible childhood. Once they have overcome their problems, they become mothers.[16] In contrast, girls who are destroyed by the sexual aggression they have suffered and who are told that they will never recover from their wounds have problems when they become mothers.[17]

Direct observation of how they look after their

children, together with questionnaires, sheds light on their inner world and reveals one constant: their low self-esteem makes them over-permissive. 'I'm not competent. My husband, my sister and the doctor are better at it than I am. I'll let them get on with it, and I'll give my child everything and not stop her from doing anything, so that she will be free to blossom. It costs me dear but that doesn't matter because she will be happy.' A small group of forty-five children who were victims of incest was followed up by means of interviews and observed in standardized situations until they became parents. A second group of 717 children who had not been abused was followed up and observed in the same way. On the whole, the population of the children of victims who had not been repaired displayed the same behavioural disorders and the same damaged self-image as children whose parents were alcoholics, mentally ill or who had themselves been traumatized.[18] They just stared at their babies, and were intimidated by their own children. Their self-esteem was poor and they expressed a utopian desire to become perfect.

Children who grow up with parents like this learn to be somewhat condescending towards the mothers who are so anxious to be their servants and the self-effacing fathers who do everything they ask and work in secret so as not to bother their little darlings with their wretched adult problems.

When they are old enough to have sex, their parents cannot give them any security because they themselves are still damaged. Because they are so anxious not to hold back their children, they do not spell out clearly what is taboo. This lack of clarity disturbs adolescents and sometimes even leads to anxious inhibitions because saying that something is taboo makes adolescents feel secure, provided that they are also clear about what is permissible. 'Taboos' are often confused with prohibitions, but the two things organize very different worlds. Prohibition blocks all expressions of desire, whereas taboos give them a form and can even orient them. 'You can express your aggressiveness up to a certain point, but beyond that point it is taboo. You can pay court to this woman, but not that one, and not just in any old fashion: you cannot do just what you like.' Taboos give the drives a shape and promote emotional coexistence, whereas prohibitions imprison desire.

Damaged parents who have not been helped to become resilient invest too much in their partners, in society and in their own children. They give in to their children so as not to hold them back and thus teach them to dominate their nice parents by letting them think they are weak. Such emotional misunderstandings are common when traumatized parents find resilience work difficult. It takes thirty years for incest victims to dare to talk about the aggression they suffered. The deportees spoke out only when their culture invited them to do so forty years after the end of the Second World War. The 200,000 children born to French women and German soldiers during the war are only now beginning to write the last chapters of their biographies, and have until now always concealed the darkness from whence they came.

A parent who has not been fully repaired finds it difficult to understand what a child really is and what a child does because no one has told them about these things. It is behaviour that mediates in the emotional misunderstandings that occur between damaged parents and their children. When a mother who was the victim of incest thirty years ago realizes that her daughter is experiencing the first stirrings of sexuality, she becomes even more fearful and over-protective. But the same mother will say nothing when her son begins to become interested in sex.[19] Not a word is said during these behavioural transactions, which take place without the partners in the scenario being aware of what is going on. The mother is only dimly aware of the obscure forces that make her smother her daughter with her intrusive surveillance and exasperating devotion, whereas her son is astounded by her extreme permissiveness, which he often interprets as meaning he can do whatever he likes: 'I can do what I like. I don't have to sit my exams when I'd rather go out on the pull.' In some cases, the child will interpret a parent's self-effacement as meaning that he has been abandoned: 'I can do what I like; in any case, my mother doesn't give a damn.' The misunderstanding is complete.

The sexual awakening of their children reawakens painful memories for mothers who were raped and betrayed as girls. What takes place in the real world takes on different meanings and organizes different behavioural transactions, depending on the parent's history. That is why adults who were abused as children are often relieved when their own children reach adolescence. It is almost as though they were thinking: 'He's too big to be abused now, that's a relief. I've won. I haven't abused him the way I was abused.' These tacit parental hints arouse feelings which, when they are expressed, organize behavioural transactions. It is as though their gestures and facial expressions were alluding to something that cannot be talked about: 'I'm worried about my daughter's sexual awakening because it reminds me of the time I was raped. I have to protect her . . . My son's interest in sex frightens me and is forcing me to be even more self-effacing.' We also hear parents saying: 'Now that my children are adolescents, I'm no longer afraid that the abuse will be repeated and our relationship is much better.' When someone has a history, facts cannot not be interpreted.

Talking About the Past to Stop It Returning

We therefore cannot say that aggression suffered in childhood is the only predictor of parental behaviour, as a damaged parent may become either intrusive or self-effacing, over-protective or detached, sombre or cheerful, depending on how his or her representation of the trauma evolves. And that is why resilience is so powerful. It is because we can modify our representations by talking about them, sharing them or influencing those around us and our culture, that we know that we feel differently about them. A wound inflicted in the past may become bearable if the representation of it can be reworked: 'I'm no longer ashamed of having failed my exams; in fact I'm quite proud of the fact that I started my own business and have people who went to top universities working for me.' We must, however, be careful as this ability to evoke the past can also bring the suffering back.

Thanks to literature, Georges Perec succeeded in overcoming the childhood loss he experienced when his family disappeared. His father joined the Foreign Legion in 1939: he disappeared. His mother went with him to the Gare de Lyon: she disappeared in the Nazi camps. There was no mourning and no psychotrauma. They simply disappeared, one after the other. The boy was lost and confused because he no longer had any attachment-figures to make him want to go on living. He was shattered and remained in that numb state until he resolved to become a writer so as to give his parents a proper burial by talking about them in his books. This reawakened the child, who studied to be an archivist and then became a novelist. And then one day, a publisher asked him to write about his childhood.[20] After a few weeks of work, Perec was so badly affected by the return of the trauma that he had to stop writing.

Resilient memories do not bring back suffering; on the contrary, they transform it and use it to produce a novel, an essay or some form of commitment. This work of representation, which makes the past undergo a metamorphosis and allows us to control our feelings, is very different from the return of the past, which brings back the suffering. If we wish to write about the past without bringing back the trauma, we have to integrate the work of memory into a project, an intention or a daydream. When we do that, 'Writing is a way of confronting the object's absence, and the energy that goes into any creative project is drawn from the source of the trauma.'[21] Georges Perec wrote in order to establish a relationship with the dead. Creating the new bond was therefore a source of comfort and the fact that *A Void (La Disparition)* was a huge literary success must have amused him greatly.* Jorge Semprun followed the same path when, after a long silence during which speaking or writing was a threatening reminder of death, he published a novel entitled *The Disappearance* (*L'Evanouissement*) at almost the same time.[22] The resilience effect consists in 'committing oneself to the work of writing [in order to] confront a situation that includes a relationship with an absent third party'.[23] Resilient writing establishes a new bond with the dead, and does not ruminate about past sufferings.

Is it the way we talk about it and the way our statements are organized that gives a representation the power to make the transition from shame to cheerfulness, from trauma to resilience? 'I remember that when I was about seven or eight, she [my mother] decided to talk to us, briefly and soberly, about the dangerous times she had been through. I soon began to have nightmares. I kept seeing jack-booted Germans coming into the house, smashing up everything and taking my parents away by force. I used to hide away to cry and then, when I was eleven or twelve, I began to read up on the subject. It made a big impression on me.'[24] It is not the actual trauma that is passed on. It is the psychotrauma, or its representation. If that is the case,

---

* *A Void* was written without use of the letter 'e', which is the central letter of 'mère' and 'père'.

and if it is true that we perceive the world only through the mirror we hold up to it, why can't we move so as to alter its image? 'Those who died in the Holocaust were not just victims. They may also have been gods on an altar. At the time, my staple diet was the fantasy that I would have liked to have been a deportee . . . whenever I saw an old man with a tattoo on his arm, I thought it suited him. I'd have liked to have been in his place so that I too could be an object of admiration.'[25]

Marriages of Despair

We have to try to understand the apparent contradiction between the trauma that exists inside our heads and the psychotrauma that is an object of admiration.

The young people who came back from the death camps married in haste as soon as they had come back to life. These early survivor marriages have been described as 'marriages of despair'.[26] The many studies that have been devoted to them stress the extreme sensitivity of these couples, emphasize how painfully easy it was for any recent event to remind them of how they had suffered, and look at the long-term effects of all that chaos. Their children had to grow up with parents who were still damaged, and as a result they had to take responsibility for their elders at a very early age. They resented their weakness. Can we say that the trauma has been passed on to them? Or would it be more accurate to say that these children adapted to the darkness they could see in their attachment-figures?

Studies of these children are very contradictory. Some contend that the children of Holocaust survivors are biologically damaged, that their cortisol levels are high, and that the most banal alert will make them feel great stress.[27] Other scientists demonstrate, on the contrary, that these children, who were raised to be icons, were 'memorial candles', and that their parents became emotionally dependent on them.[28]

Attachment theories can provide other answers[29] by combining a large number of different approaches such as the Adult Attachment Interview (the way in which adults evoke their emotional relations with their parents), studies of anxiety levels, levels of biological stress, the scale of the impact of events, questions relating to mourning and unresolved traumas, criteria for social observation and direct observation of styles of childcare.

It transpires from this enormous body of work that

- young Holocaust survivors had many fewer representations of secure attachment (23 per cent) than the control groups (65 per cent);

- there were far more cases of unresolved mourning;
- the difficulties were definitely not passed on to their children.

What does this mean?

It means that personal interviews are more coherent than the findings of scientific research. Everyone was surprised to find that these young survivors were so successful. But if we talk to them about their subjective lives, we quickly discover that their emotional lives are disordered and that the schematic clarity of social adventurism was the only thing that put them at their ease. In their heart of hearts, they experienced great sorrow. In order to stop themselves thinking that no one could love the living corpses they had become, that they exuded unhappiness and that they would communicate their unhappiness to those who deigned to love them, they took refuge in the only activity that prevented them from suffering. When they could do that, the rules of life were clear, and all they had to do was get up early, go to bed late and think of nothing but work. All they needed to follow the narrow path that led to social success was their courage. They ceased to suffer, and even found a certain peace, but the pain was never far away. They were saddened by their own emotional incompetence, and by their inability to say 'Mum', to be tender, to invent family rituals, to hold little parties or friendly gatherings at which their family could share a cake or a story. 'My mother used to make the same cake.' How could they be expected to use such nice banalities when they'd never had either a mother or a cake? They thought they could compensate for their disordered attachment and the difficulty they had in expressing the confused love they felt by working hard in order to be able to give a lot. They gave their gifts in secret because they had not mastered the rituals of giving presents. Some of them did very well at school, even though they had not been allowed to go to school during the war. Many of them were very successful, much to the surprise of people who, after an uneventful childhood in a loving family, found it difficult to acquire a few qualifications at school.

I can just hear the cynics saying: 'So you're saying that if you want a child to do well at school, you should stop her from going to school, and if you want someone to do well in life, you have to lock them up in a death camp!' My answer to that is to say that these young survivors experienced a morbid success. They worked and studied like mad because that lessened their suffering and because they were repairing their self-image and learning to hope once more. Their morbid success illustrates the splitting mechanisms that somehow allowed them to become at least a little stronger as they stood on the edge of the emotional precipice. They could not love until a partner gently taught them to acquire the secure attachment that almost all of them (77 per cent) had lost. That is why these 'marriages of despair' were so full of hope. They allowed a lot of traumatized individuals to repair their self-image and then to learn slowly how to establish a peaceful bond. These couples' children were born in the middle of a parental repair shop. They became attached to parents who were split, brave and touchy, who were socially strong and emotionally vulnerable and who invested far too much in their children. For their part, the children felt they were being dominated and, in some cases, despised by their successful parents. 'They achieved social success in terrible circumstances, and yet they gave me everything. They must despise me. But I still think they are weak.'

Emotional misunderstandings are common in these families. Not talking about the horrors they have suffered is the parents' way of protecting their children and of not passing on the trauma that is still there inside their heads. But because they use splitting mechanisms to lessen their sufferings and to repair themselves, they imprint an ambivalent attachment on the souls of their children.

Is It the Way We Talk About It That Passes On the Trauma?

We do not have to go on mourning the unburied dead for ever, provided that, once the din has died down, our social and emotional environment allows us to get on with our resilient development once more. The little Armenian, Jewish and Rwandan orphans did not descend into a pathological mourning when the context allowed them to find surrogate families. Establishing new bonds allowed them to come back to life and, in some cases, gave them a pathological courage. Their resilience got to work and gradually allowed them to find peace.

The children of these traumatized adults were learning to become resilient, but they had to deal with adults who were socially cheerful and emotionally gloomy. Splitting, which is a legitimate defence mechanism, and adaptation to aggression do not in themselves foster resilience but they do prevent both the damaged parents and their children from feeling any pain. If the children who were hidden had not been able to keep quiet about their origins, they would have died. If, after the war, they had revealed their dark side too soon, they would have passed on the psychotrauma to their children. Without realizing it, they gave them an ambivalent emotional style which, paradoxically, protected them. It was thanks to that costly mechanism that, as adults, survivors' children are no different from the control groups.[30] One in three displays an insecure attachment, but the same is true of the population at large. This means that first-born children, who are more ambivalent, improve as they get older and meet other people, whereas their younger siblings are able to grow up with parents who have already been repaired. The damaged adults and their eldest children are forced to undertake the resilience work that taught them to love 'like everybody else', but they do so at a later stage than everybody else.

Secure and confused emotional styles are the most easily passed on.[31] We are, however, talking about tendencies and not destiny, and a confused attachment is not irredeemable. Helping the damaged parents to repair themselves is all it takes to prevent the distress from being passed on. A psychotrauma is passed on only when the family situation or cultural context builds an emotional prison in which the damaged parents are left alone with their children and pass it on directly. Adults pass on their psychotraumas (their notions of what happened to them) only when they are in a relationship based upon a fusional attachment that cuts them off from the world.

After the war, the young survivors spared their families and children their suffering through denial, splitting and morbid courage. They paid a very high price, but they also got a good bargain because those who did not pay this exorbitant price either passed on their psychotrauma or went on feeling guilty because they had survived. In La Seyne, which is where I work, the Communists displayed great bravery during the Second World War. Some of them took part in the Liberation with Leclerc's army after it landed in Provence. Many were shot because of their involvement in the Resistance and others came back from the camps determined to bear witness. They talked, held commemorative meetings, distributed photographs and constantly brought to life the horrors of the incredible persecution they had suffered. They were never in denial and they did not metamorphose their sufferings because they were so eager to proclaim the abomination of Nazism.

Their children had to grow up with a daily representation of the nightmare. Their parents remained intact, did not use splitting mechanisms and were always brave and committed to ensuring that 'it must never happen again'. Their children internalized a world that had been invaded by death, torture and fear.

Those adults who were in denial refused to see what the real trauma meant: 'Oh, that's all over now . . . Life goes on. Stop moaning; we didn't have an easy time of it either.' Splitting occurs because of 'the coexistence within the psyche of two groups of phenomena – or even of two distinct personalities each of which may know absolutely nothing of the other'.[32] Because their personalities were disordered, these parents did not pass on their psychotrauma, but that does not mean that they passed on nothing. Their curious personalities, their intense intellectualism and their strong but ill-expressed emotions led their children to form ambivalent attachments. Their children admired but feared their parents, and sometimes despised them because their relational skills were so poor.

The wounded parents who refused to remain silent in order to fight Nazism more effectively sometimes passed on their psychotrauma by enveloping their children in an intolerable representation. The split parents, in contrast, protected their children by keeping silent. They taught them an ambivalent style of attachment, but that is one of the most malleable styles and it can easily be modified by acting upon the representations conveyed by the narratives they heard around them.

'Most deportees waited until their children were adolescents before telling them about their deportation.'[33] Before that, they talked to their partners, their in-laws or a few close friends, but even the clearly enunciated statements they made in the presence of their children could not enter their psyches because they meant nothing to them. It was not that the children were in denial. They were afflicted by a sort of psychical deafness that made it impossible for them to take in information that had no meaning. 'I've just seen a kapo* I used to know in Auschwitz.' When overheard by a child of under ten, the phrase had much the same meaning as 'I've just seen the grocer I used to know in Bénodet. He's closed his shop. It had a funny effect on me.' The expression was not worth storing in their memory and could not become part of the identity of the child who heard its father use it.

When, on the other hand, these children reach adolescence and become old enough to be socialized, the words 'Auschwitz' and 'kapo' are pregnant with meaning. At that age, such phrases alert the child, provided that the verbal parent–child relationship has been sustained until adolescence, which is not always the case, provided that his partner has not forced her wounded husband to keep quiet because she does not want to be upset, provided that his family and friends are interested in what he has to say, and provided that his culture allows the wounded to speak – it often asks them to remain quiet so as not to disturb its tranquillity. When their stories can be talked about openly, 'one descendant in two says they heard about it as a

---

* A prisoner, usually a criminal, who was a guard or trustee in a Second World War concentration camp.

child . . . and the others "got to know" in early adolescence,' but '20 per cent of all descendants have never been able to talk about it'.[34]

From Shame to Pride

The early ambivalent attachment has, then, moved on when the adolescent, who has now been socialized, suddenly takes an interest in the wounds that were inflicted on his or her parent. By the time the descendants of the wounded have become adults, most of them have resolved their ambivalence thanks to their first love, and the way they view their parents' suffering has changed.

In this population of descendants, we find that 87 per cent of children are proud of their parents, who were either deported or killed because they were in the Resistance or the army. Their parents' war records gave the children a representation of which they could be proud, even when it was not talked about openly. The child imagines: 'My father joined the Foreign Legion. He was mentioned in dispatches before they arrested him on his hospital bed.' Even when the representation remains private, the child knows that he will be able to talk about it in these terms one day.

The stories about his parents that the adolescent stages in his subjective theatre give rise to feelings that can be modified by cultural activities, political discourses, philosophical essays and works of art. That representation may change as the adolescent's interests change: 'I wasn't interested. It frightened me and bored me, but I am now fascinated by learning about my parents' difficult story.' Like characters in some Greek tragedy, they had to survive incredible ordeals. They projected their enigmatic shadow on to me, and that turned me into a hesitant child. I was dreamy and I had no choice about becoming an intellectual. I became a psychoanalyst so as to be able to transform their suffering into a sublime story, into a narrative, by understanding the hidden side of our condition: 'I was proud of my inheritance, proud that they both passed this difficulty on to me. That question that is still unresolved and that has made me stronger . . . and proud of my name.'[35]

The inevitable changes that take place in cultural narratives and in the child's interests, and the working-off mechanisms used by the wounded, explain the astonishing ease with which those who suffered traumas can establish a dialogue with their grandchildren.[36] As time goes by, they make good progress with the resilience process, and campaign to change personal and social representations. Their grandchildren are therefore spared the ambivalent effects of the traumatic memory. The relationship is more transparent, the bond is lighter and both parties enjoy talking to each other. Yes, 'enjoy': people who were wounded enjoy the fact that, now that they have become resilient, they no longer have to admit to their shame and suffering. They tell their grandchildren about how they defeated the abomination of Nazism, and their grandchildren are delighted to have a wonderful grandmother who beat the baddies and became so kind. Siegi Hirsh said: 'That was the first time I didn't tell my grandchildren that the number on my arm was a telephone number. I explained to them, and now I can talk to them as a grandfather.'[37]

The first child of traumatized parents was born when they were still bleeding. Their younger children were less affected by the trauma their parents had suffered, but they were affected by their silent conflicts. They all sensed the presence of the shadow, of the worrying enigma that borders on anguish, but which can also be an invitation to enjoy the delights of 'archaeological digs'. Many of these children have become artists. Others, like novelists or psychoanalysts, have discovered crypts or explored the depths. Their journeys into inner worlds have given them both the pleasant tiredness that comes from making an effort, and the pleasures of discovery that resolved their ambivalence. The resilience process of the children of resilient parents has given the grandchildren creative parents and wonderful grandparents. Whereas the psychotrauma forced them to change because the only alternative was a psychic collapse, resilience invites them to go through the metamorphosis that transforms wounds into strength, and shame into pride.

All this is far removed from the linear causalities in which one agency has effects that grow worse over the generations. In resilience theories, the subject is influenced by a constellation of determinants. As a result, he or she struggles and intentionally looks for the tutors that will allow him or her to begin to develop once more.

We Do Not Have to Pass On Our Unhappiness

This is why the example of the deportees' children is, perhaps, a little too clear: Evil is on one side, and Good eventually triumphs, just as it does in the moral of a folk tale. But what do abused children who want to protect the fathers who are brutalizing them have to do to become resilient? What will happen to the childhood victims of incest who experience both pleasure and shame?[38] Their trauma is made worse because the categories are unclear and because society often abuses them for a second time by refusing to believe that their nice fathers could do such a thing.

Children who were hidden during the war rubbed shoulders with death every day. A neighbour could have been denounced with just one word that meant nothing to them. An SS man could have shot them dead just because they looked at him. Their torments were real, but they knew where the danger lay, and they knew who was protecting them. The Devil was embodied in a social ideology, and the Righteous amongst the Nations saved them with their affection. After the war, there were a lot of intra-familial adoptions. Some foster families repaired the children, but others did quite the opposite. Many children were unable to go back to school; they received no grants because they could not produce their parents' death certificates and because, having learned to keep quiet in order to stay alive, they still kept quiet in peacetime. Because they were trying to hide such a monstrosity, they looked strange and became even more isolated.

Many war orphans had never known a more nerve-racking situation. If they were lucky enough to have established the first links in a secure attachment before the catastrophe, and before their parents were suddenly taken away from them, they remained loyal to that image and continued to develop a healthy attachment to a dead parent.[39] The bond was perfect because their dead parents could not make any mistakes as they brought them up. Children like this were eager to obey their dead parents' wishes. When a neighbour or an archive revealed the ambitions their deceased parents had for them – 'When she gave birth to you, your mother said: "He will become a doctor"' – the revelation gave the posthumous project a power that was non-negotiable. The attachment remained ideal and transcended death, and that intergenerational mandate gave the child a transcendent mission. This explains the morbid successes that our culture admires so much.

We do not have to pass on our unhappiness. Some never recovered from the blow they suffered, but those who did fight it discovered an inner world that was like an oxymoron: 'Although they were devastated by the horrors they had witnessed . . . [they also] felt that a miracle had saved them.'[40] The second generation grew up with parents who were still busy with their resilience work. 'Deafened by the din of what was not being said . . . and staring into a void haunted by ghosts',[41] they survived by learning to decipher enigmas and to repair mental worlds. They were so good at it that the third generation could re-establish family ties by discovering the pleasure of questioning the first generation, which really did suffer in the past.

It is impossible not to pass on something. Physical proximity is all it takes. This soul-to-soul communication can, however, pass on happiness as easily as it can pass on unhappiness. A trauma casts a shadow, but the stories that are told about it bring princesses out of the darkness as well as toads. That is why fairy tales are so powerful. That is the difficult hope that is promised by resilience.

VII

Conclusion

I knew Mr Superman well. I was his psychotherapist for a long time. He was suffering from a serious fate neurosis which had convinced him that his life was governed by an invisible power that made him rush to the rescue of anyone who was in danger. This repeated constraint gave Mr Superman the feeling that he was, despite himself, experiencing 'the periodic recurrence of identical chains . . . of events'.[1]

Mr Superman was very badly affected by his neurosis.

It was a dream that allowed him to find an explanation for this periodic recurrence of events. When he was a little orphan in an anonymous institution, he was astonished to wake up to realize that he had often had a dream in which he had only to raise his arms and pedal his legs as though he were riding a bicycle to rise gently into the air. When he had been unhappy during the day, he dreamed of this ecstatic liberation at night. But he felt sad when he awoke because coming down to earth brought him back to a real world in which there was no hope. In order to make his non-existence less painful, he would contrive to get himself into difficult situations that let him feel he was living a little. The hold of the past was so strong that it made him repeat what he had learned.

Mr Superman was not happy. As he grew older, a defence mechanism that had had its uses when he was a child became a fate neurosis that forced him to repeat scenarios he no longer needed. 'I find unhappiness uplifting,' he said sadly. 'I look for situations in the real world that make me feel that I'm alive. As soon as the spectacular action is over, the return to everyday life confirms that my days are empty, and I try to give them a meaning by performing a few feats.' It is these ordeals that give the ego its ability to keep us alive in the face of danger,[2] he added, with some bitterness. Having developed this life strategy, he experienced a strange pleasure when he undertook this defensive manoeuvre and wondered where this unusual constraint came from. At the time, he did not know that fate enslaves those who believe in their own fantasies.

He therefore had to escape from this defensive strategy which had, in its day, protected Mr Superman because it was trapping him in the past.

A traumatic wound numbs us rather than torturing us. So much so that some wounded people give the impression that they are strangely indifferent. Sándor Ferenczi reports wounded soldiers as saying that they were no longer in any pain and had ceased to exist.[3]

The most comfortable solution is to stay dead, and that is the solution that our culture finds easiest to expect. 'After what he's been through, well, what do you expect? He's screwed.' Too much compassion condemns us to a psychic death and if, by some mishap, you fight to come back to life, there's a danger that you will cause a scandal. 'What? He's dancing! He was happy on his way back from the cemetery!' Wearing mourning for a long time makes us look virtuous, and merry widows often have a bad reputation. Someone whose soul has been wounded can look moral only if they suffer constantly. If they are unlucky enough to get over it, they take a more relativist view of the aggressor's crime. Resilience is suspect, don't you think?

It is not unusual for someone who has come back to life to be judged in this way, as the gravity of the crime is thought to be proportional to the gravity of its effects. I have the impression that, in societies that are still under construction, we identify with the aggressor, admire the strength of people who get their own way and who know how to make their social conceptions triumph. In established societies, we look virtuous and democratic when we identify with the victim of the aggression. Because we lead such comfortable lives, we can afford the luxury of claiming to share the sufferings of the wounded and that makes us feel good about ourselves.

Mr Superman illustrates this way of living in a culture where the poor and the needy suddenly demonstrate that they are not that weak after all: they can rush to the rescue of someone who is being attacked without losing their humble status. Our hero demonstrates how those who are unfairly treated can be the dispensers of justice.

Resilience is a third way that avoids both identification with the aggressor and identification with the victim of the aggression. The goal of a resilience process is to discover how we can come back to life without repeating the aggression or making a career of our victim status. At the time of the accident they all – absolutely all of them – say, 'I'd like to be like everyone else again.' And when some of them begin to emerge, they all – absolutely all of them – say, 'I've been very lucky, you know.' This is the very opposite of the ideology of the superman, which implicitly contains the ideology of the subhuman.

Resilience attempts to answer two questions:

- How is it possible to hope when there is no hope? Studies of attachment provide one answer.
- How did I manage to survive? Research into personal, family and social narratives explains how we can modify our representations.

Someone who is wounded cannot come back to life immediately. It is hard to dance when your legs have been broken. When we collapse we have to remain under an anaesthetic for a while so as to calm down and to begin to hope again. The psychic feeling of numbness we get when we have just been hurt explains why we go into denial when we have witnessed something terrible: 'Yes, I was caught up in a terrorist attack. Some people died and people were screaming all around me. I was badly burned. So what? I fought in the Algerian war and lived to tell the tale!' There is no conflict when we think like this. It is just that other people don't understand. 'A large part of my psyche has been scarred. So what? Life goes on!'

If we walk too soon after we have broken a leg, we make the fracture worse, and if we speak too soon, the wound stays open. But, sooner or later, we have to stop living with death and, if we are to find a little happiness, we really do have to break free from our wounded past. So we act, commit ourselves to some project, talk about something else or write a story in the third person so as to express ourselves and to distance ourselves from the past sufficiently to regain control over our emotions and to regain possession of our inner worlds.

We take our first steps on the long road to resilience when the din dies down, and as soon as a spark of life brings new light into a world that suddenly went dark. When we reach that point, we cease to be psychically dead and begin the task of living once again.

It so happens that when we fall in love and embark on a relationship, we go through a sensitive period because we re-enact our past. We commit everything we have acquired to our relationship in order to make our dream of a new life come true. 'Why should anyone love me?' That question is basic to any relationship. It is also basic to the implicit understanding that organizes a relationship by giving it its style.

Mechanical miracles occur every day, over every breakfast and with every 'good night'. The miracles and the richness of banality weave a new bond and bring a new life into the world.

> And yet it still has to sing
> I may be no more than a cry . . .
> Listen to yourself weeping inside
> Over stories of times gone by
> The terrible seeds they sowed
> Ripen from poem to poem
> The revolts that have begun.[4]

It is the poet's privilege to be able to say in a few lines what it has taken me 260 pages to say.

Notes

1 Introduction

1 E. Rostand, 'C'est dans la nuit qu'on croit à la lumière' in Catherine Schmutz-Brun, *La Maladie de l'âge*, FAPSE, University of Geneva, Colloque de Fontrevraud, 22 May 2003.

2 B. Hoerni, *L'Archipel du cancer* (Paris: Le Cherche-Midi, 1994), p. 54.

3 F. Chapuis in J. Alessandri, 'A Propos de la résilience', Mémoire pour le diplôme universitaire de victimologie (Paris: Université René-Descartes, 1997), p. 25.

4 A. Jollien, *Eloge de la faiblesse* (Paris: Cerf, 1999).

5 P. Gutton, personal communication, Journées de psychanalyse autour de Jean Laplanche, 'Le Crime sexuel', Aix-en-Provence, 27 April 2002.

6 René A. Spitz, 'Anaclitic Depression', *Psychoanalytic Study of the Child*, 2, 1946, pp. 313–42.

7 See René A. Spitz, *The First Year of Life* (New York: International Universities Press, 1958).

8 Joseph Sandler, *The Analysis of Defense: The Ego and the Mechanisms of Defense Revisited* (New York: International Universities Press, 1985).

9 John Bowlby, *Attachment and Loss*, vol. 1, *Attachment* (London: Pimlico, 1997); vol. 2, *Separation: Anger and Anxiety* (London: Pimlico, 1998); vol. 3, *Loss: Sadness and Depression* (London: Pimlico, 1998).

10 P. Aulagnier, *L'Apprenti-historien et le maître-sorcier* (Paris: Presses Universitaires de France, 1984).

11 See John Bowlby, 'Development Psychiatry Comes of Age', *American Journal of Psychiatry*, 145, 1988, pp. 1–10.

12 Primo Levi, *If This Is a Man/The Truce*, translated by Stuart Wolf (London: Abacus, 1987), p. 35.

13 C. de Teichey in M. Anaut, 'Trauma, vulnérabilité et resilience en protection de l'enfance', *Connexions*, no. 77, 2002, p. 106.

14 G. de Gaulle-Anthonioz, Preface to G. Tillion, *La Traversée du canal (Entretiens avec Jean Lacouture)* (Paris: Arléa, 2000).

15 'A Bâtons rompus avec Germaine Tillion', *Le Patriote résistant*, no. 21, April 2000.

16 J. Guillaumin, *Entre Blessure et cicatrice* (Syssel: Champ Vallon, 1987), pp. 196–8.

II *Resilience as Anti-Destiny*

1 Jean-Luc Godard, *Eloge d'amour* (film, 2001), Film Reminiscence.

2 G. Haldas, *Mémoire et résurrection* (cited in substance) (Lucerne: L'Age d'homme, 1991), pp. 167–8.

3 I have already used this example elsewhere. See Boris Cyrulnik, *Sous le Signe du lien* (Paris: Hachette, 1989), pp. 225–6.

4 D. L. Schacter, *A la recherche de la mémoire* (Brussels: De Boeck Université, 1999).

5 Maria Nowak, *La Banquière de l'espoir* (Paris: Albin Michel, 1994), p. 108.

6 Ibid., p. 126.

7 J. Gervet, *Eléments d'éthologie cognitive* (Paris: Hermès Sciences Publications, 1999), pp. 47–61.

8 It appears to be a false memory, as the Charles Péguy Association has not been able to trace the quotations. I may have been thinking of William James, who remarks somewhere in his *Principles of Psychology* that mental life is above all purposeful.

9 P. Karli, *Le Cerveau et la liberté* (Paris: Odile Jacob, 1995), pp. 303–6.

10 Alfred Adler, *What Life Could Mean to You*, edited by Colin Brett (Oxford: One World, 1989), p. 12.

11 Z. Laidi, *Le Sacré du Présent* (Paris: Flammarion, 2000) in N. Aubert, 'Le Temps des urgences', *Cultures en mouvement*, no. 59, August 2003.

12 Norman Sartorius, addressing the international IFOTES congress, Ljubljana, Slovenia, July 2003. Cf. Norman Sartorius, *Fighting for Mental Health* (Cambridge: Cambridge University Press, 2002).

13 V. E. Frankl, *Découvrir un sens à la vie* (Montréal: Les Editions de l'homme, 1993), p. 161.

14 L. Marin, *De la Représentation* (Paris: Seuil, 1994), p. 169.

15 Ibid.

16 P. de Roo, *Mécaniques du destin* (Paris: Calmann-Lévy, 2001), p. 19.

17 J. Hatzfield, *Dans le nu de la vie. Récits du marais rwandais* (Paris: Seuil, 2000), p. 161.

18 *La Gazette des tribunaux*, 11–12 January 1892, cited in G. Vigarello, *Histoire du viol* (Paris: Seuil, 1998), p. 231.

19 'Sainte Thérèse d'Avila' in P. de Roo, *Mécaniques du destin*, op. cit.

Notes

III *When a Meeting Is a Reunion*

1 'Sensitive period: a moment in the life of an organism when it becomes particularly amenable to certain learning processes. During an ontogenetic period, certain environmental influences leave a more stable or lasting impression than an equivalent or more powerful experience that occurs outside this phase.' K. Immelman, *Dictionnaire de l'éthologie* (Brussels: Mardaga, 1990).

2 K. R. Merikangas and J. Angst, 'The Challenge of Depressive Disorders in Adolescence' in M. Rutter (ed.), *Psychosocial Disturbances in Young People* (Cambridge: Cambridge University Press, 1995), pp. 131–65.

3 A. C. Petersen, B. E. Compas, J. Brooks-Gunn, M. Stemmler, S. Ey and K. E. Grant, 'Depression in Adolescence', *American Psychologist*, 48, 1993, pp. 155–8.

4 B. Ambuel, 'Adolescents' Unintended Pregnancy and Abortion: The Struggle for a Compassionate Social Policy: Current Directions', *Psychological Science*, 4, 1995, pp. 1–5.

5 See John Bowlby, *Attachment and Loss*, vol. 1, *Attachment* (London: Pimlico, 1997); vol. 2, *Separation: Anger and Anxiety* (London: Pimlico, 1998); vol. 3, *Loss: Sadness and Depression* (London: Pimlico, 1998).

6 R. Miljkovitch, 'L'Attachement au niveau des représentations' in N. Guedeney and A. Guedeney, *L'Attachement: Concepts et applications* (Paris: Masson, 2002), pp. 27–8.

7 A. Guedeney, 'De la réaction précoce et durable de retrait à la dépression chez le jeune enfant', *Neuropsychiatries de l'enfant et de l'adolescent*, 47 (1–2), 1984, pp. 63–71.

8 B. Egeland and E. Farber, 'Infant–Mother Attachments:

Factors Related to its Development and Changes over Time', *Child Development*, 55 (3), 1999, pp. 753–71.

9 J. Lecomte, *Guérir de son enfance* (Paris: Odile Jacob, 2004), p. 42.

10 Margaret H. Hicks, 'The Social Transformation of Parental Behaviour: Attachment Across Generations' in I. Bretherton and E. Waters (eds.), *Growing Points of Attachment Theory and Research* (Monographs of the Society for Research in Child Development, 1985), 50 (1–2), p. 227.

11 Catherine Enjolet is currently trying to set up an association that can give children who are in difficult circumstances a similar kind of relational gift: 'Parrain par mille', 25 rue Mouffetard, 75005 Paris.

12 R. L. Paikoff, S. Brook and J. Gunn, 'Physiological Processes: What role do they play during the Transition to Adolescence?' in R. Montemayor and G. R. Adams, *A Transitional Period?* (Newbury Park, CA: Sage, 1990), pp. 63–81.

13 P. C. Racamier, *L'Inceste et l'incestuel* (Paris: Collège de psychanalyse groupale et familiale, 1995): 'the imprint of non-fantasized incest, even if it is not necessarily committed in the genital sense.' Trying on his mother's underwear or the pleasure of finding his parents playing erotic games can make a child scent a whiff of incest.

14 H. Freeman, 'Who Do You Turn To: Individual Differences in Late Adolescent Perception of Parents and Peers as Attachment Figures' (thesis, University of Wisconsin, 1997) in F. Atger, *Attachement et adolescence* (Paris: Masson, 2002), pp. 127–35.

15 H. Bee and D. Boyd, *Psychologie du développement. Les âges de la vie* (Brussels: De Boeck Université, 2003), pp. 197–9.

16 J. E. Fleming, 'Prevalence of Childhood and Adolescent

Depression in the Community. Ontario Health Study', *British Journal of Psychiatry*, 15, 1989, pp. 647–54.

17 P. Jeammet, 'Les Risques de décompensation dépressive à l'adolescence et la démarche préventive' in C. de Tichey, *La Prévention des dépressions* (Paris: L'Harmattan, 2004).

18 R. Miljkovitch, 'Attachement et psychopathologies durant l'enfance' in N. Guedeney and A. Guedeney, *L'Attachement: Concepts et applications*, op. cit.

19 J. P. Allen and D. J. Land, 'Attachment in Adolescence' in J. Cassidy and P. Shauer (eds.), *Handbook of Attachment: Theory, Research and Clinical Implications* (New York: Guilford Press, 1999), pp. 595–624.

20 B. Cyrulnik, 'De l'Attachement à la prise de risque' in J.-L. Venisse, D. Bailley and M. Reynaud (eds.), *Conduites addictives, conduites à risques: quels liens, quelle prevention?* (Paris: Masson, 2002), pp. 75–81.

21 B. Cyrulnik in M. Versini (ed.), 'Les Enfants de la rue', UNESCO Colloquium, 25 January 2002.

22 J. Waldner, 'Le Placement en institution' in J.-P. Pourtois (ed.), *Blessure d'enfant* (Louvain: De Boeck Université, 1995), p. 253.

23 On the theory of imprinting, see Boris Cyrulnik, *Sous le Signe du lien* (Paris: Hachette, 1989); *Les Nourritures affectionels* (Paris: Odile Jacob, 1991); *Les Vilains Petits Canards* (Paris: Odile Jacob, 2001); F.-Y. Doré, *L'Apprentissage, une approche psycho-éthologique* (Paris and Québec: Maloine, 1983).

24 D. Bauman, *La Mémoire des oubliés* (Paris: Albin Michel, 1988), pp. 205–6.

25 M. Lemay, 'Les Difficultés sexuelles de l'adolescence', *Psychiatries* 6, no. 64, 1984, pp. 57–64, and 'Carences primaires et facteurs de risque de dépression postnatale

maternelle' in C. de Tichey, *La Prévention des dépressions*, op. cit.

26 A. F. Valenstein, 'Une Fille devient femme: le caractère unique du changement de l'image de soi pendant la grossesse' in E. J. Anthony and C. Chiland, *Prévention en psychiatries de l'enfant en un temps de transition* (Paris: Presses Universitaires de France, 1984), p. 135.

27 M. Silvestre, 'Pathologie des couples', Cours de diplôme d'université, Toulon, 17 January 2004.

28 State or act of desiring; appetite; craving. Strong sexual overtones.

29 E. Werner and S. Smith, *Vulnerable but Invincible* (New York: McGraw Hill, 1982).

30 C. Garcia, L. M. Reza and A. Villagran, 'Promoción de resiliencia en niñas y jóvenes con antecedentes de abandono y maltrato' (Tijuana, Mexico: Aldea Infantil SOS, 2003).

31 Elizabeth Roudinesco, Preface to Jenny Aubry, *Psychanalyse des enfants séparés* (Paris: Denoël, 2003), p. 26.

32 On these experiments, see Boris Cyrulnik, *Sous le Signe du lien*, op. cit.

33 Jenny Aubry, *La Carence de soins maternels* (Paris: Presses Universitaires de France, 1955).

34 Ibid.

35 John Bowlby, 'Developmental Psychiatry Comes of Age', *American Journal of Psychiatry*, 145, 1988, pp. 1–10.

36 Discussion about street children with a South American Minister for the Family, as reported by Marie-Rose Moro.

37 Michael Rutter, 'Parent–Child Separation: Psychological Effects on the Children', *Journal of Child Psychology and Psychiatry*, vol. 12, 1971, pp. 233–60.

38 Charles Dickens, *Oliver Twist* (London: Everyman's Library, 1960), p. 21.

39 J.-M. Perier, *Le Temps d'apprendre à vivre* (Paris: XO, 2004), p. 92.

40 Louis Aragon, 'Il n'y a pas d'amour heureux' in *La Diane française* (Paris: Seghers, 1946).

41 M. David, 'Le Placement familial: de la pratique à la théorie' (Paris: ESF, 1989), p. 44.

42 Boris Cyrulnik, *Le Murmure des fantômes* (Paris: Odile Jacob, 2002), pp. 110–14; J.-F. Legoff, *L'Enfant, parent des ses parents* (Paris: L'Harmattan, 2000).

43 J. Plaquevent, *Le Premier droit de l'enfant* (Paris: De Fallois, 1996), pp. 109–19.

44 John Bowlby, *Attachment and Loss:* vol. 2, *Separation: Anger and Anxiety*, pp. 278–9, citing C. B. Stendler, 'Possible Causes of Overdependency in Young Children', *Child Development*, 25, 1954, pp. 125–46.

45 J. Newson and E. Newson, *Four Years Old in an Urban Community* (Chicago: University of Chicago Press, 1968).

46 Sigmund Freud, *Three Essays on the Theory of Sexuality*, in *On Sexuality* (The Pelican Freud Library, vol. 7) (London: Penguin, 1977), p. 146.

47 John Bowlby, *Separation: Anger and Anxiety*, op. cit., p. 282.

48 D. Marcelli, *L'Enfant, chef de famille. L'Autorité de l'infantile* (Paris: Albin Michel, 2003), pp. 254–7.

49 S. Lesourd, '"La Passion de l'enfance" comme entrave posée à la naissance du sujet', *Le Journal des psychologues*, no. 213, January 2004, pp. 22–5.

50 J.-P. Chartier and L. Chartier, *Les Parents martyrs* (Toulouse: Privat, 1989).

51 Boris Cyrulnik, 'Les Muets parlent aux sourds', *Le Nouvel Observateur*, January 2004 (special issue on 'La Mémoire de la Shoah').

52 Kiyoshi Ogura, 'Alternance de séduction, de symbiose et d'attitudes meurtrières des enfants japonais envers leur mère: syndrome d'une ère nouvelle?' in E. J. Anthony and C. Chiland, *Prévention en psychiatries de l'enfant en un temps de transition*, op. cit., pp. 319–25.

53 Ibid., p. 323.

54 M. C. Holzman, Journées de l'UNICEF, Paris, 7 April 1996.

55 G. Wahl, *Epsylon*, Labos Boots-Darcour, no. 4, 1989.

56 M. J. Paulson, R. H. Coombs and J. Landverk, 'Youths who Physically Assault their Parents', *Journal of Family Violence*, 5, Part 2, 1990, pp. 121–33.

57 S. Honjo and S. Wakabayashi, 'Family Violence in Japan: A Compilation of Data from the Department of Psychiatry, Nagoya, 1978, cited in M. Dugas, M.-C. Mouren and O. Halfen, 'Les Parents battus et leurs enfants', *Psychiatrie de l'enfance*, 28, 1985, pp. 185–220.

58 B. Cyrulnik, A. Alameda and P. Reymondet, 'Les Parents battus: de la séduction à la soumission', in M. Delage, *Congrès des neurologues et des psychiatres de la langue française*, Toulon, 14 June 1996.

59 A. Laurent, J. Boucharlat and A.-M. Anchisi, 'A Propos des adolescents qui agressent physiquement leurs parents', *Annales médico-psychologiques*, vol. 155, no. 1, 1996.

60 C. Delannoy, *Au Risque de l'adoption. Une Vie à construire ensemble* (Paris: La Découverte, 2004), p. 88.

61 L. Keltikanga-Jarvinen, 'Attributional Style of the Mother as a Predictor of Aggressive Behaviour of the Child', *Aggressive Behaviour*, vol. 1, 1990, pp. 1–7.

62 C. Delannoy, *Au Risque de l'adoption*, op. cit., pp. 89–90.

63 Ian Kershaw, *Hitler 1889–1936: Hubris* (London: Penguin, 1999), p. 9.

64 Ibid., p. 12.

65 Ibid., p. 9.

66 Ibid., p. 12.

67 Ibid.

68 Ibid.

69 Ibid., p. 18

70 Ibid., p. 16.

71 J. Guillaumin, *Entre Blessure et cicatrice: Le Destin du négatif dans la psychanalyse* (Seyssel: Champ Vallon, 1987), p. 191.

72 A. Marthur and L. Schmitt, 'Epidémiologie de l'ESPT après un traumatisme collectif', *Stress et trauma*, 3 (4), 2003, p. 216.

73 J. Bergeret, *La Violence fondamentale* (Paris: Dunod, 1985).

74 Guillaumin, *Entre Blessure et cicatrice*, op. cit, p. 198.

75 Sigmund Freud, letter of 1 August 1919 to Lou Andreas-Salomé, cited in Peter Gay, *Freud: A Life for Our Time* (London: Papermac, 1989), p. 394 and note, p. 703.

76 Bowlby describes this image as an 'Internal Working Model'.

77 A. Guedeney, 'De la réaction précoce et durable de retrait à la dépression chez le jeune enfant', *Neuropsychiatrie de l'enfant et de l'adolescent*, 47 (1–2), 1999, pp. 63–71.

78 C. Hazan and P. Shaver, 'Attachment as an Organization Framework for Research on Close Relationships', *Psychological Inquiry*, 5, 1994, pp. 1–22.

79 R. C. Schank and R. P. Abelson, *Scripts, Goals and Understanding* (Hillsdale, NJ: Erlbaum, 1977).

80 M. Mancia, 'Dream Actors in the Theatre of Memory: Their Role in the Psychoanalytic Process', *International Journal of Psychonalysis*, 84, 2003, pp. 945–52.

81 Sigmund Freud, 'Analysis Terminable and Interminable', *The Standard Edition of the Complete Psychological Works of Sigmund Freud* (London: The Hogarth Press and the Institute of Psychoanalysis, 14 vols, 1953–73), vol. XXIII, p. 252.

82 J.-C. Kaufmann, *L'Invention de soi. Une théorie de l'identité* (Paris: Armand-Colin, 2004), p. 153.

83 Jeremy Holmes, *John Bowlby and Attachment Theory* (London and New York: Routledge, 1993).

84 E. Bibring, 'The Concept of the Repetition Compulsion', *Psychoanalytic Quarterly*, XI, 4, 1953, p. 502.

85 V. de Gaulejac, *Les Sources de la honte* (Paris: Desclée de Brouwer, 1996), p. 225.

IV The Metaphysics of Love

1 Imaginary letter from a former adolescent boy.

2 O. Bourguignon, 'Attachement et détachement' in D. Houzel, M. Emmanuelli and F. Moggio, *Dictionnaire de psychopathologie de l'enfant et de l'adolescent* (Paris: PUF, 2000), pp. 70–72.

3 Ph. Gutton, 'La Parentalité', seminar, Aix-en-Provence, 8 March 2004, citing D. Lagache and P. Mâle, 'Arguments pour un symposium psychanalytique sur l'adolescence: les relations avec autrui et les relations avec soi-même', *Rapport du i^{er} congrès européen de pédo-psychiatrie* (Paris: SPEI, 1960), pp. 205–7.

4 R. Miljkovitch, *L'Attachement au cours de la vie* (Paris: PUF, 2001), pp. 196–231; Boris Cyrulnik, *Sous le Signe du lien*, op. cit., pp. 244–52.

5 M. D. S. Ainsworth, 'Some Considerations Regarding Theory and Assessment Relevant to Attachment Beyond Infancy' in M. T. Greenberg, D. Cicchetti and E. M. Cummings (eds.), *Attachment in the Preschool Years: Theory, Research and Intervention* (Chicago: University of Chicago Press, 1990).

6 Mihal Ioan Botez (ed.), *Neuropsychologie clinique et neurologie du comportement* (Montréal: Presses de L'Université de Montréal, 1987), p. 93.

7 A. R. Damasio, *Spinoza avait raison. Joie et tristesse, le cerveau des émotions* (Paris: Odile Jacob, 2003), pp. 118–19.

8 R. L. Birdwhistell, *Kinesics and Context* (Philadelphia: University of Pennsylvania Press, 1970).

9 N. Dobriansky-Weber, 'La Parade nuptiale: une histoire sans paroles', *Le Journal des psychologues*, 139, July–August 2003, p. 23.

10 Boris Cyrulnik, *Les Nourritures affectives* (Paris: Odile Jacob, 1993), pp. 17–49; I. Eibli-Eibesfeldt, *Ethologie: biologie du comportement* (Paris: Editions Scientifiques, 1972), pp. 428–52.

11 P. Lemoine, *Séduire. Comment l'amour vient aux humains* (Paris: Robert Laffont, 2004).

12 H. Bee and D. Boyd, *Psychologie du développement. Les âges de la vie*, op. cit., p. 298; M. Odent, *The Scientification of Love* (London: Free Association Books, 1999).

13 J. Lecomte, *Guérir de son enfance* (Paris: Odile Jacob, 2004).

14 H. Elder, 'The Life Course as a Developmental Theory', *Child Development*, 69 (1), 1998, pp. 1–2.

15 'Les Caractéristiques de la population sexuellement active', *La Recherche*, 223, July–August 1990; M. Bozon and H. Leridon, *Sexualité et sciences socials* (Paris: PUF, 1995).

16 R. Neuburger, *Le Mythe familial* (Paris: ESF, 1995).

17 Johann Wolfgang von Goethe, *The Sorrows of Young Werther*, translated by Michael Hulse (London: Penguin, 1989), p. 37. Cf. P.-L. Assoun, 'Le Trauma amoureux. Le "Complexe de Werther"', *Le Journal des psychologues*, 159, July–August 1998.

18 P.-M. Crittenden, 'L'Evolution, l'expérience et les relations d'attachement' in E. Habimana, L. S. Ethier, D. Petot and M. Tousignant (eds.), *Psychopathologie de l'enfant et de l'adolescent* (Montréal: Gaëtan Morin, 1999), pp. 86–8.

19 Ibid., p. 90.

20 Sigmund Freud, *The Interpretation of Dreams* (The Pelican Freud Library, vol. 4) (London: Penguin, 1976), pp. 719–20.

21 John Bowlby, *Attachment and Loss*, vol. 1, *Attachment*, op. cit.

22 M. Delage, B. Bastien-Flamain, S. Baillet-Lucciani and L. Lebreton, 'Application de la théorie de l'attachement à la compréhension et au traitement du couple', *Thérapie familiale*, 2 (2), 2004.

23 M. T. Greenberg and M. L. Speltz, *Contribution of Attachment Theory to the Understanding of Conduct Problems during the Preschool Years* (Hillsdale, NJ: Erlbaum, 1988).

24 P. Fonagy and N. Target, 'Attachment and Reflexive Function: Their Role in Self-Organization', *Development Psychopathology*, 9, 1997, pp. 679–700.

25 B. Pierrehumbert, A. Karmanolia, A. Sieye, R. Miljkovitch and O. Halfon, 'Les Modèles de relation: développement d'un autre questionnaire d'attachement pour adultes', *Psychiatrie de l'enfant*, vol. 1, 1966, pp. 161–206.

26 This was done by giving a one to ten rating to four columns of questions inspired by the adult attachment questionnaire

designed by Blaise Pierrehumbert (Lucerne). Each column corresponded to: secure attachment, ambivalent attachment, avoidant attachment and distress.

27 B. Cyrulnik, M. Delage, S. Bourcet, M.-N. Blein and A. Dupays, 'Apprentissage, expression et modification des styles affectifs après le premier amour' (unpublished).

28 C. Duchet, C. Jehel and J.-D. Guelfi, 'A Propos de deux victimes de l'attentat parisien du RER Port-Royal du 3 décembre 1996: vulnérabilité posttraumatique et résistance aux troubles', *Annales medico-psychologiques*, 158 (7), 2003, pp. 539–48.

29 M. Gannagé, *L'Enfant, les parents et la guerre. Une Etude clinique au Liban* (Paris: ESF, 1999).

30 M. Declerq, 'Les Répercussions du syndrome de stress posttraumatique sur les familles', *Thérapie familiale*, 16 (2), 1995, pp. 185–95.

31 A. M. Blanc, 'Les Femmes dans la protection maternelle et infantile: une problématique de la place de la femme dans la société actuelle', thèse du troisième cycle, UFR sciences sociales, Aix-Marseille-I, January 2000.

32 G. E. Armsden, E. McCawley, M. T. Greenberg and P. M. Burke, 'Parent and Peer Attachment in Earlier Adolescence and Depression', *Journal of Abnormal Psychology*, 18, 1990, pp. 683–97.

V Inheriting Hell

1 R. Robinson, 'The Present State of People who Survived the Holocaust as Children', *Acta Psych. Scand.*, 89, 1994, pp. 242–5.

2 M.-P. Poilpot (ed.), *Souffrir mais se construire. Fondation pour l'enfance* (Ramonville Saint-Agne: Erès, 1999).

3 E. Bouteyre, *Réussite et résiliences sociales chez l'enfant de migrants* (Paris: Dunod, 2004).

4 M. Main, N. Kaplan and J. Cassidy, 'Security in Infancy, Childhood and Adulthood: a Move to the Level of Representation' in I. Bretherton and E. Waters (eds.), *Growing Points of Attachment Theory and Research, Monographs of the Society for Research into Child Development*, 50 (1–2; Serial no. 290), 1985, pp. 66–104.

5 M. Gilbert, *L'Identité narrative* (Geneva: Labor et Fidès, 2001), p. 37.

6 M. D. Ainsworth, M. C. Blehar, E. Walters and S. Wall, *Patterns of Attachment Assessed in the Strange Situation at Home* (Hillsdale: Erlbaum, 1978).

7 B. Cyrulnik and F. Cyrulnik-Gilis, 'Ethologie de la transmission des désirs inconscience. La Cas "Pupuce"', *Evolution psychiatrique*, vol. XLV, fasc. III, 1980, pp. 553–66.

8 I. Boszormenyi-Nagy and J.-L. Framo, *Psychothérapies familiales* (Paris: PUF, 1980).

9 B. Golse, 'Transgénérationnel' in D. Houzel, M. Emmanuelli and F. Moggio, *Dictionnaire de psychopathologie de l'enfant et de l'adolescent*, op. cit., p. 743.

10 D. Stern, 'Intersubjectivité, narration et continuité dans le temps', Journées SFPEADA, 'La Communication et ses troubles', Caen, 14 May 2004.

11 Ricks (1985), Grossman (1988), Fonagy (1991), Ward (1995), Main (1996), Zeanah (1996).

12 P. Fonagy, 'Mental Representations from an Intergenerational Cognitive Science Perspective', *Infant Mental Health Journal*, 15, 1994, pp. 57–68.

13 C. Mareau, 'Mécanismes de la résilience et exploitation

sélective des compétences au sein d'une relation mère-enfant potentiellement pathogènes', Thèse de doctorat, Université Paris-V, June 2004.

14 See D. W. Winnicott, *Collected Papers: Through Paediatrics to Psychoanalysis* (London: Tavistock, 1958).

15 P. Fonagy, M. Steele, H. Steele, G. S. Moran and A. C. Higgit, 'The Capacity for Understanding Mental States: The Reflective Self-Parent in Mother and Child and its Significance for Security of Attachment', *Infant Mental Health Journal*, 12 (3), 1991, pp. 201–18.

16 P. Brenot, *Le Sexe et l'amour* (Paris: Odile Jacob, 2003).

17 Letter to the author (2003), cited in substance. I have received several anonymous letters like this, which suggests that several of the children who were so unfairly damaged have been able to become psychiatrists.

18 M. Delage, 'Traumatisme psychique et résilience familiale', *Stress et trauma*, 2 (2), 2002, pp. 69–78.

19 M. Rubenstein, *Tout le monde n'a pas la chance d'être orphelin* (Paris: Verticales, 2002).

20 Ibid., p. 85.

21 P. Benghozi, 'L'Attaque contre l'humain. Traumatisme catastrophique et transmission généalogique', *Nervure*, vol. IX, no. 2, March 1996.

22 E. Mujawayo and S. Belhaddas, *SurVivants* (La Tour d'Aigues: Editions de l'Aube, 2004), p. 149.

VI *Sombre Songs*

1 P. Benghozi, 'Porte-la-honte et maillage des contenants généalogiques familiaux et communautaires en thérapie

familiale', in *Revue de psychothérapie psychanalytique de groupe* (Paris: Erès, 1994).

2 Dialogue based upon J.-C. Snyder, *Voyage de l'enfance* (Paris: PUF, 2003), pp. 23–5.

3 A. de Mijolla, *Préhistoires de famille* (Paris: PUF, 2004), p. 150.

4 J. Snyder, *Voyage de l'enfance*, op. cit., p. 108.

5 Ibid., p. 123.

6 S. Parent and J.-F. Saucier, 'La Théorie de l'attachement' in E. Habimana, L. Ethier, D. Petot and M. Tousignant, *Psychopathologie de l'enfant et de l'adolescent* (Montréal: Gaëtan Morin, 1999), p. 30.

7 J. Lighezzola and C. de Tyychey, *La Résilience. Se (re)construire après le traumatisme* (Paris: In Press, 2004), p. 72.

8 Jeremiah 31: 30.

9 C. Trevarthen, P. Hubley and L. Sheeran, 'Les Activités innées du nourrisson', *La Recherche*, no. 6, 1975, pp. 447–58.

10 Mary Main, 'Cross-Cultural Studies of Attachment Organization. Recent Studies: Changing Methodologies and the Concept of Conditional Strategies', *Human Development*, 35, 1990, pp. 48–61.

11 John Bowlby, *A Secure Base: Clinical Applications of Attachment Theory* (London: Routledge, 1998), pp. 33–5.

12 N. Guedeney and A. Guedeney, *L'Attachement: Concepts et applications*, op. cit., p. 30.

13 J. Lecomte, *Guérir de son enfance*, op. cit., p. 200.

14 A. Boutros-Boutros Galli, Cité de la Réussite, Forum de l'écrit, Paris, 19 June 2004.

15 M. Frydman, *Le Traumatisme de l'enfant caché* (Quorum, 1999).

16 W. Kristberg, *The Invisible Wound: a New Approach to Healing Childhood Sexual Trauma* (New York: Bantam Books, 1993).

17 C. A. Curtois, *Healing the Incest Wound: Adult Survivors in Therapy* (New York: W. W. Norton, 1998).

18 A. M. Ruscio, 'Predicting the Child-Rearing Practices of Mothers Sexually Abused in Childhood', *Child Abuse and Neglect*, 25, 2001, pp. 362–87.

19 C. Krellwetz and C. C. Piotrowski, 'Incest Survivor Mothers: Protecting the Next Generation', *Child Abuse and Neglect*, vol. 22, no. 12, 1998, pp. 1305–12.

20 Georges Perec, *A Void*, translated by Gilbert Adair (London: Harvill Press, 1996). The French original (*La Disparition*) was published in 1969.

21 A. Aubert, 'La Diversion, voie de dégagement de l'expérience de la douleur' in F. Marty, *Figures et traitements du traumatisme* (Paris: Dunod, 2001), p. 224.

22 Jorge Semprun, *L'Evanouissement* (Paris: Gallimard, 1967).

23 André Green, *La Déliaison. Psychanalyse, anthropologie et littérature* (Paris: Hachette Littérature, 1973).

24 S. Landau-Mintz. The manuscript deserves to be published.

25 M. Rubenstein, *Tout le monde n'a pas la chance d'être orphelin*, op. cit., pp. 102–3.

26 Y. Danieli, 'Families of Survivors of the Nazi Holocaust: Some Short- and Long-Term Effects in Stress and Anxiety' in I. G. Spielberger, N. Y. Sarason and C. D. Milgram (eds.), *Hemisphere*, vol. 8 (New York: McGraw Hill, 1981).

27 R. Yehuda, J. Schmeidler, A. Elkin, S. Elson, L. Siever, K. Binder-Brynes, M. Fainberg and A. Aferiot, 'Phenomenology and Psychobiology of the Intergenerational

Response to Trauma' in *International Handbook of Multi-generational Legacies of Trauma* (New York: Plenum, 1998).

28 Z. Solomon, M. Kotler and M. Mikulinger, 'Combat-Related Post-Traumatic Stress Disorder among Second-Generation Survivors: Preliminary Findings – American', *Journal of Psychiatry*, 145, 1997, pp. 865–8.

29 S. Sagi-Schwartz, M. Van Ijzendoorn, K. E. Grossman, T. Joels, K. Grossman, M. Scharf, A. Koren-Karie, A. Alkalay, 'Les Survivants de l'holocauste et leurs enfants', *Devenir*, vol. 16, no. 2, 2004, pp. 77–107.

30 Ibid.

31 M. H. Van Ijzendoorn, 'Association between Adult Attachment Representations and Parent–Child Attachment, Parental Responsiveness and Clinical Status. A Meta-Analysis of the Predictive Validity of the Adult Attachment Interview', *Psychological Bulletin*, 117, 1995, pp. 387–403.

32 J. Laplanche and J.-B. Pontalis, *The Language of Psychoanalysis*, translated by Donald Nicholson-Smith (London: The Hogarth Press and the Institute of Psychoanalysis, 1973), p. 427.

33 C. Breton, 'Socialisation des descendants de parents résistants déportés de France', Doctorat de sciences de l'éducation, Université Paris-X-Nanterre, 1993, p. 370.

34 Ibid., pp. 371, 390.

35 P. Grimbert, *Un Secret* (Paris: Grasset, 2004), pp. 177–8.

36 P. Fossion, M. C. Rejas, L. Servais, I. Pelc and S. Hirsch, 'Family Approach with Grandchildren of Holocaust Survivors', *American Journal of Psychotherapy*, vol. 57, no. 4, 2003.

37 M. Heireman, 'Le Livre des comptes familiaux' in Patrice Cuynet (ed.), *Héritages* (Paris: L'Harmattan, 1999), p. 84.

38 N. de Saint-Phalle, 'Honte, plaisir et peur . . .' in *Mon Secret* (Paris: La Différence, 1944), p. 8.

39 R. C. Fraley and P. R. Shaver, 'Loss and Bereavement: Attachment Theory and Recent Controversies Concerning "Grief Work" and the Nature of Detachment' in J. Cassidy and P. Shaver (eds.), *Handbook of Attachment* (New York: Guilford Press, 1999).

40 F. Castaignos-Leblond, *Traumatismes historiques et dialogue intergénérationnel* (Paris: L'Harmattan, 2001), p. 196.

41 Ibid.

VII *Conclusion*

1 J. Laplanche and J.-B. Pontalis, *The Language of Psychoanalysis*, op. cit., p. 161.

2 A. Aubert Godard, 'Fondements de la santé, triade et traumas originaires' in F. Marty (ed.), *Figures et traitements du traumatisme*, op. cit., p. 26.

3 See Sándor Ferenczi, 'Gedanken über das Trauma', *International Zeitschriften für Psychoanalyse*, 5, no. 20, 1934, pp. 5–12.

4 Louis Aragon, 'Le Malheur dit' in *Le Fou d'Elsa* (Paris: Gallimard, 'Poésie', 1963), pp. 365–8.